T0367590

No-Fail Retail

Merchandising Techniques for Stores

REGINA BLESSA

NO-FAIL RETAIL
MERCHANDISING TECHNIQUES FOR STORES

iUniverse books may be ordered through booksellers or by contacting:

iUniverse
1663 Liberty Drive
Bloomington, IN 47403
www.iuniverse.com
1-800-Authors (1-800-288-4677)

Because of the dynamic nature of the Internet, any web addresses or links contained in this book may have changed since publication and may no longer be valid. The views expressed in this work are solely those of the author and do not necessarily reflect the views of the publisher, and the publisher hereby disclaims any responsibility for them.

ISBN: 978-1-4917-5634-8 (sc)
ISBN: 978-1-4917-5636-2 (hc)
ISBN: 978-1-4917-5635-5 (e)

Library of Congress Control Number: 2014922798

Print information available on the last page.

iUniverse rev. date: 11/20/2015

CONTENTS

Presentation xiii
   The Power of Retail Marketing xiii
Introduction xv

CHAPTER 1: Merchandising 1
   Merchandising: Some Concepts 1
      Main Functions of Merchandising 2
      How to Visually Explain Merchandising 3
   Merchandising Techniques 4
      Product Supply 4
      Pricing 9
      Position 14
      Access 21
      Displaying 23

CHAPTER 2: Visual Merchandising 29
   The Rigors of Visual Merchandising 30
   Highlights of Basic Visual Merchandising 31
   Windows 34
   Ambiance 41
   Purchasing Atmosphere 42
      What is the Purchasing Experience? 42
      What Composes a Good Atmosphere? 43
      Knowing What In-Store Atmosphere to Use 43
      How to Create a Buying Atmosphere 44
   The Human Perception According to Senses 44
   The Buying Experience and the Five Senses 45
      Sight 46
      Hearing 47
      Smell 47
      Taste 48
      Touch 49
   Color Sensations 50
   Light 51

How Can I Use This Knowledge in My Store? 52
    Design Project..53
    Store Planning 53
Visual Design is as Important as Price............................54
    Oral..55
    Climatic 56
    Gustatory...56
    Visual..56
    Sound 57
    Aromatic 57
    Signage 57
    Proxemics..58

CHAPTER 3: The Store 59
  Location 60
    Details...61
    Traffic and Parking 62
    Visibility 62
    Compatibility with the Area......................................63
    Neighborhood and Competition..............................63
    Rent and Extra Costs 63
  Store Floor Plan 64
  Store Layout 66
  External Store Image 69
  Exterior Design..69
    The Storefront..70
    The Entrance...70
    The Window Display...72
    Impellers..73
  Interior Design...75
    Inside the Store 75
    Sales Area 77
    Identifying the Hot Areas..77
    Product Displays...78
    Circulation 78
    How to Use Store Space 81
  Store Operation 83
    Logistics...83

CHAPTER 4: The Gondola 85
    Gondolas 85
    Shelves 87
    Gondola Arrangement 87
        Vertical 89
        Horizontal 90
        Blocky 91
        Self-Service Product Positioning 93
    Endcaps 94
    Counters 96
    Stacking 97
    Pallets 98
    Cleaning 98
    Managing Spaces 98
    Planogram 100
        Creation of Planograms 100
        Planogram Purpose 101
        Making and Keeping a Planogram 102
    How Categories Boost Sales 106
        How Categories Changes by Retail Type 107
    Retail Is Detail 107
    What does a well-displayed product mean for you? 109

CHAPTER 5: Promotional Marketing 110
    Promotional Actions 110
    Promotional Environment 110
    Planning and Implementation 111
        Demand 111
    Conducting Promotions 112
    Types of Promotional Actions for Suppliers and Retailers 112
        Suppliers Helping Train Retail 112
        Relationship 113
        Education and Interaction for Consumption 113
        Loyalty Actions 114
        Motivating Actions 114
        Couponing 114
        Incentive 115
        Institutional 115
        Cultural 115

Demonstration 116
Tasting.. 116
Sampling... 117
Cross Sampling 117
Giveaways or Promotional Bundles............... 117
Store Flyer Promotions 119
Actions in the Packaging............................... 119
Cooperative Advertising 119
Contests and Sweepstakes 119
Looking for Customers Outside the Store........................ 120
Selling Spaces for Actions in POP............................ 120
How to Improve Promotional Actions...................... 121

CHAPTER 6: Understanding Customer Perception 122
Memory 122
Understanding.. 123
Loyalty.. 123
Brand Identity.. 123
Brand Experience... 123
The Brand and the POP: A Two-Way Street 124
Visual Perception 124
Consumer Vision.. 125
Scanning Shelves in Seconds 126
Memorization and Generalization............... 126
Product Positioning.. 128
The Perception of Product Brand and Store Brand.......... 128
Packaging 129
The Challenge of Attracting the Consumer 133

CHAPTER 7: Customer Care.. 134
Customer Service... 134
Word of Mouth and Negative Image............................ 135
How to Enchant the Consumer.................................... 135
Customer-Centric Retailing.............................. 137
First Impressions Are the Most Lasting 137
Learn Which Customers
Should Receive Special Treatment 138
Know Your Audience 139

Women's Buying Power 140
   Women Make Key Purchasing Decisions 140
Employees versus Consumer.. 141
   Contact with People 141
Promotional Work Force 142
   Benefits to Retailers 142
   Personal Profile for the POP Worker........................ 143
   Functions of Merchandisers.. 144
   Checklist for Professional Skills Training................. 144

CHAPTER 8: The Point of Purchase as Media............................ 146
   Promotional Material.. 147
   How to Create Good In-Store Material.......................... 147
   Basic Criteria for Obtaining Maximum Efficiency
      with the POP 148
   Advantages of Materials... 149
   Impact of Materials... 149
      Types of Displays and Their Uses 152
   Communication with the Consumer.............................. 160
   ROI: Return on Investment.. 161
   Shopper Marketing versus In-Store Marketing.......... 161

CHAPTER 9: The Psychology of Consumption 163
   The Economic Theory of Consumption 163
   Behavior of Consumption 165
   Most Mass-Merchant Purchase Decisions Are In-Store.... 166
   Persuasion during the Purchase 167
   Types of Purchase Decisions.. 167
   Self-Service and Hands-On Experience 169
   Invisible Barriers that Block the Impulse 170
   Behavior during Purchases 172
   What May Affect the Buying Habits?............................. 172
   Purchase Procedures at POPs... 173
   The difference between consumers and shoppers............ 173
   Pre-store and in-store marketing 173

CHAPTER 10: Trends in Global Retail 175
   Eye-Tracking Research 175
      The Consideration Set 176
      Eye Tracking and Consideration Set 177
      Considerations in an Eye-Tracking Study 179
      The Type of Shopping Trip Influences Impulse
         Purchases 179
      Store Appearance Drives Shopper Attitude 181
      Shelf Placement Drives Purchases 181
      Leading Brands Do Well in Shelf Blocks 182
   The Future of Omni-Channel Retailing 184
      Big Data 184
      Showrooming 184
      Webrooming Eclipses Showrooming 185

Conclusion 187
References 190
Author Information 194

To my mom and dad,
now watching over me from the second floor.

PRESENTATION

When we think about *point of purchase*, the first thing that comes to mind is location—that is, the commercial space and its interior. However, these are no more the basic elements that must be prepared properly if we hope to invite consumers into our stores and convince them to buy and come back. Any discussion of modern merchandising must extend far beyond the simple elements of fixtures and communication; it must explore all available opportunities to create an ongoing, successful business and build a history of consumer loyalty.

Our brain receives around 11 million bits per second; however we are able to process only 40 percent of everything we see. Depending on the category, 60 to 90 percent of shopping decisions are taken at the POP in front of the gondola; also, we know that 50 percent of these decisions happen on "autopilot", when the consumer decides what to pick, taking an average of fifteen seconds scanning the gondola, focusing only 5 seconds on the product or the promotional material.

Learning how to use merchandising techniques and control the everyday experience at the POP requires an ongoing strategy. In a simple, streamlined way, this book will show retailers and students alike the necessary elements for achieving an effective merchandising strategy that will boost sales and attract more customers.

The Power of Retail Marketing

The point of purchase is the place where sales are made. On the macro level, it may be a mall, market, or street. On the micro level, it is the area surrounding the counter where retail customers pay, also known as "point of sale." In recent years, the POP for products and services has become an important focus for marketers, because that's where consumers tend to make most of their purchasing decisions. Points of purchase may be tangible, as in the case of a brick-and-mortar store, or virtual, as in the case of a retailer that sells goods and services on the Internet.

When combined with its marketing actions and the trade marketing actions of industry, retail is one of the most powerful global commercial forces.

But suppliers should know that, in the end, it is the retailer who controls which of their products looks better on store aisles and which of their messages or in-store materials are transmitted to their consumers.

It is up to us to simultaneously administer each piece of a merchandising effort or promotional action so that both the industry and the retailer sides always profit from the union.

With the frenetic pace of daily life, consumers are obliged to buy as wisely and as quickly as possible. While shopping is a necessity for them, they won't waste their time paying attention to a commercial message unless it is strong, visible, and succinct.

The biggest global companies that arose from strong brands and merchandising campaigns have already noticed that the influence of in-store materials cannot be ignored. They know that the successful campaign's main event is the sale.

The store is not a lone vehicle. We know that in market planning, merchandising is the most critical factor, because it's at the time of purchase that the consumer's money changes hands.

Inside stores, the battle for consumers is becoming harder. Media fragmentation, the increasing quantity of products, online shopping, retail consolidation and sophistication, and ongoing changes to consumer's behavior, lifestyles and demographics have combined to bring big changes to the way products and services are commercialized.

Nowadays retail marketing has become an extremely important component in the marketing mix.

INTRODUCTION

Retailer-consumer communication is vital to obtaining more and better results from merchandising, reinforcing a store's image, products, and brands. More than anything else, consumers needs to interact with the product and with the point of purchase, to feel present and engaged in a space totally dedicated to their well-being and needs.

In the retail universe it is also important to know how to use actions and work with the intermediate public (the people between the supplier and the consumer) so that the result is synergic and helps create an identity. Gradually, suppliers and retailers together will try to shape a brand or product image, as they become more aware of the importance of this image to customer loyalty.

In some countries, merchandising starts with the purchasing plan and uses complex consumption mathematics to determine the entire life of each item or collection to be sold. In other countries, the purchasing and merchandising processes are completely separate: merchandising is responsible only for the product's life inside the store and its essential presentation to the consumer. In both cases, however, there must be a constant evolution of the merchandising tools used in communication. Merchandisers must develop new strategies for attracting and seducing consumers, working with all the senses to create the perfect product ambiance at the point of purchase.

Above all, the POP represents the moment and place of convergence for all the elements that make a sale: the product, the consumer, and the money. Retailers, therefore, need to be up-to-date on market demand, watching their team professionalism, customer relations, price and stock strategies, merchandising and ambiance, customer service, and communication through the media.

For this reason, retailers have been more receptive to merchandising programs offered by the big suppliers at the point of purchase. A store is ultimately responsible for sales flow, and controlling sales flow is only possible for retailers who know how to make the best of merchandising. Don't forget that the time of purchase can be the first or the last, crucial moment when retailers talk to consumers.

When we talk about the market—about what happens between industries, retailers, dealers, and consumers—we understand that we are all part of a cycle that generates products for the population to consume. In this cycle, which manufacturing industry creates and produces, there is a hard and long path until reaching the consumer. After a product is finalized in the manufacturing process, it is handed over to marketing, which will largely be responsible for planning its life cycle. While marketing uses research to develop a successful product launch, advertising develops a plan to present the product and information about it to its target audience. Before any marketing or advertising communication is released to the media, the point of purchase must be prepared to complete the cycle that will result in a purchase. There is no point in spending millions on advertising if proper preparations have not been made at the retail level. When it's time for the consumer to make a purchasing decision, the store and its staff must be ready to offer the consumer the result of all this marketing effort.

Production-consumption cycle: *Every element of a marketing plan converges at the point of purchase, where the product finally meets the shopper. Merchandising is responsible for the most critical part of marketing.*

The production-consumption cycle will be completed only if the consumer understands the message and finds the product displayed at the store.

When we pay more attention to advertising than to merchandising, and consumers get to the stores and don't find the products that were advertised, we won't just be missing a few sales. We'll be throwing away all the money spent on manufacturing, advertising agency and media, serving up our customers on a platter to our competitors.

In order to be effective, merchandising cannot be used only on occasion; its techniques must be applied constantly at the point of purchase, because it is a vital part of good daily contact with the consumer.

Merchandising is the most critical part of marketing because it is where consumers and products meet.

Here are the principal marketing tools:

- **Advertising** informs and tries to influence the consumer about the product through various communication vehicles during product launch. It also gives product support and helps in difficult sales moments.

- **Promotion** activates and accelerates product turnover through promotional actions, with or without the use of media, on specific and strategic occasions.

- **Merchandising** is responsible for featuring products in the store, creating space and increasing visibility in a way that accelerates product turnover.

- **Visual Merchandising** augments the retail design of a store. It is one of the final stages in setting out a store in a way customers find attractive and appealing.

- ***Trade marketing*** is the bridge between a company's commercial (sales) and marketing areas. It oversees the development of plans and commercial strategies to increase sell-in and sell-out negotiations with the retailer. It is the job of the trade marketing team to increase demand from both shoppers (in-store marketing) and supply chain partners (such as distributors, wholesalers, and retailers), rather than at the consumer level.

Placed with the sales team at most companies, the trade marketing team should focus primarily on the customers, with little to no focus on the shopper side (taking a customer-based, not brand- or product-based, approach). For trade marketing, success is linked to customer development and growth.

When trade marketing is placed with the marketing team (or trade marketing is the responsibility of the marketing or brand-management team), the focus is on the shopper side and the in-market (brand-based) marketing aspects. The success drivers here are linked to brand strategies (shares growth, upgrading consumers, competitor blocking, etc.).

When trade marketing is placed as a separate function all by itself, it will have a mix of customer-based and brand- or product-based approaches, and the success drivers are linked to both brand and sales strategies.

Such different placements and responsibilities can cause a lot of confusion between the sales machine and brand teams; hence, synergizing the sales and marketing plans is a key responsibility for the trade marketing team, and it's the main factor in delivering on the above definition and the company vision.

The ideal company (or perhaps the best one, as there really is no such thing as ideal), recognizes its unique nature and places trade marketing where it can function accordingly; however, the difficult part is to the set the right key performance indicators (KPIs) and expectations for trade marketing based on its placement.

CHAPTER 1:
MERCHANDISING

Merchandising: Some Concepts

Nystrom (1932) defined merchandising as "careful planning, capable styling and production or selecting and buying, and effective selling".

In the United States and some other countries, merchandisers play an important role by planning, negotiating, buying and providing products for consumption, and they analyze customer demands, understand sales trends, and know how to present the products to sell.

In some others countries, however, merchandising doesn't coordinate product planning, negotiations, acquisition, or trend analysis; it starts just at the point of purchase.

Therefore this book will only focus from this point onwards. Our merchandising begins from the store's door inside. We will focus our efforts on how a retailer that already has their products to sell should keep their store saleable from the market point of view.

The Conceptualization of Merchandising at the POP

Merchandising is any technique, action, or material used at the point of purchase to provide information about and give better visibility to products, brands, or services, with the purpose of motivating and influencing the customer's purchase decision. It is a combination of marketing and communication intended to identify, control and set the ambiance at the POP, promote brands, products, and services in retail. In short, merchandising facilitates the decision to buy.

Merchandising is a very dynamic area that is always in a state of transformation. There are many variables related to merchandising at the POP, including different instruments, techniques, and types.

Main Functions of Merchandising

- to increase impulse purchases
- to create a link between advertising and the product at the retail level
- to attract the consumer's attention
- to present the product in a more attractive way
- to better promote and identify the brand or product
- to help retail employees deal with their products
- to increase the association between a certain type of store and the product
- to help manufacturers' and dealers' sales representatives

Advantages of Merchandising for the Supplier

- improves the brand, the company, and the product's image
- creates a competitive advantage
- ensures demand for the product
- increases the product's market share

Advantages for the Supplier Salesperson and the Merchandiser

- improves the relationship between the channel and its employees
- increases sales and repeat orders
- creates opportunities for them to show their competencies

Advantages of Merchandising for the Retailer

- improves product turnover and the rate of impulse purchases
- develops the consumer's loyalty to the store
- attracts new consumers to the store
- reinforces the store's image
- increases profits

Advantages of Merchandising for the Consumer

- makes products more accessible and easily found
- helps consumers remember the products because of good displays
- makes the purchase decision quicker
- saves time because of increased convenience

How to Visually Explain Merchandising

Here we have two examples of stores—one that doesn't know how to merchandise its products, and another that has used merchandising to attract customers.

The store above seems to turn its back on customers.
The store below, on the other hand, seems to say, "Welcome, customers!"

Merchandising Techniques

Product Supply

Product supply is a very important factor in commercialization. For retailers, knowing what and when to buy is fundamental to maintaining an appropriate assortment of products that will appeal to the target consumer for price, quality, or quantity. Retailers must maintain a stock with all types of products that correspond with the preferences of their target audience, and enough of a supply to last at least a week, depending on the product.

Avoiding ruptures in supply is much more a matter of planning and inventory control than an instinct or gut feeling. Retailers must set out a minimum assortment of products and order replacements before those minimum quantities sell out. Running out of a product might seem like a small, momentary problem, but it's the easiest way to lose a customer to the competition. Not only will that one missed sale never be recovered, but the store also risks losing that customer forever to a competitor with better service. A well-supplied store with the best assortment of products does not take that risk.

Product Replacement

Replacing sold products is a store's most important job. There are no empty spaces on the shelves of the best supermarkets. A missing product is immediately replaced by another, because a space means sales, and sales means money. And while the supplier might lose market share, the store loses sales and its good reputation, because a store with empty shelves or shelves full of holes is not usually the favorite among consumers. If your store's image is damaged, not only will you lose the sales of those missing products, but you'll see your overall sales decrease.

Shortage

In retail, a shortage results in the loss of sales when customers decide to change stores because they can't find what they want in yours. Check to see which products your store needs to have and which it can do without in order to avoid ruptures.

Product Undersupply

When a product is missing in a store, consumers see it as a problem with the store, not the supplier. That is especially true when the problem frustrates their shopping habits.

An obvious rupture like this one can do a lot of damage to a store's image.

Reasons for Rupture

The store is responsible when ...
- there is an inventory error (a difference between the physical and counted stock).
- the store order is made incorrectly.
- defective or dented products are taken off the gondola and are not replaced.
- the store order is generated late.
- products are stolen from the store.
- gondolas are not refilled by the stock replenisher or the sales promoter (when the product is still in stock).
- there are problems ordering from the distribution center.
- products are placed only in promotion spots.
- products are incorrectly registered.
- there is not enough store staff to refill the shelves.

The distribution center (DC) is responsible when ...
- it does not make the correct order to the supplier.
- its order is generated late.
- product data is recorded incorrectly.
- its delivery to the store doesn't match the order.
- there is an operational error in its cross docking.
- there is an inventory problem in the DC.
- there is a delay in the delivery from the DC to the store.

The purchasing sector is responsible when ...
- the purchasing department doesn't make the correct order.
- the purchasing department decides not to proceed with the order.
- there is an inventory error in the central systems.
- price/margin negotiations with the manufacturer cause a delay.

The supplier is responsible when ...
- it does not deliver the order correctly.
- it doesn't have the requested product.
- it delays delivery.

(Supermercado Moderno Magazine. *20*)

Product Excess

Displaying a large amount of one product is acceptable only when there is a big sale with extremely attractive prices designed to stimulate customers to stock up on the product.

Displaying too many of one product for no apparent reason makes consumers assume that the store is in trouble, as too many repeated products leave room for little variety in store gondolas.

Rotation

Rotation is the technique of displaying the product with the oldest manufacture date on the front side of the shelf, and the product with the most recent manufacture date on the back. In gondola replenishment, this kind of rotation is also known as FIFO (first in, first out). When organizing stock, stores should always follow the same rotation pattern.

Common Problems when Filling Up a Store

- bad product distribution
- too many merchandisers filling up the shelves during trading hours
- too many or bad positioning of promotions
- poorly displayed products
- a lack of price tags or other information on the piles of products

See the spider?
If a product isn't selling, sometimes the problem isn't with the product.
Check its position, accessibility, and price, because unsold stock + expiration date = loss.

Pricing

When you look in a store window and don't see any price tags, what do you think? The first thing that crosses your mind is that everything must be expensive, right? Most people in that situation don't bother to go inside the store—and the same thing often happens inside the store, when people can't see the price of a product on the shelves.

Do not hide your price tag, so make it easy for the customers to know the price even without the assistance of the sales staff by putting the price tag at highly visible and expected spot.

To stick the price on the product, stick it at the upper right side of the package because eyes are naturally drawn in this area. When you use the price label holders at the shelf, prefer to affix it exactly below the product, at the same shelf the product is.

For apparel, stick the price at the neck line or collar, at the back portion of the waist line of pants or at the brand or manufacturer's tag attached on the item.

It is common for customers not to buy a product without a price tag, because during those few seconds of doubt, either they will lose the impulse to buy or they will assume that the product is very expensive and so they'll decide against buying it. Very few customers will go to the trouble of looking for the barcode reader or searching the packaging for the price. For fear of being overcharged, most consumers will leave the decision for later instead of making the purchase at that moment. Therefore, it is important that the price is properly conveyed to the consumer, because the price can decide the purchase.

Those who don't display a price if it is higher than their competitors' are losing much more than are those retailers who expose the higher price. Consumers don't keep all those prices in mind. If I asked you exactly how much you paid for the last soap you bought, would you be able to give me a precise answer?

Granted, a few people are capable of remembering the exact amount they pay for everything they buy each month; most, however, just have a notion of the average price. Either way, don't kill yourself trying to keep track of your competitors' prices. While the big chains do establish easy-to-remember prices as gimmicks to sell things like milk, Coke, bread, or other staples, they make up those lost margins with their other products. Only customers who have extra time and not much money look for good deals on all products. We call these people "bargain hunters" or "bottom feeders"; they are capable of spending ten dollars in fuel to save fifty cents on a product.

Price Offer

The biggest stimulator of the impulse purchase is the price offer. If the price is advantageous to the customer, it should be written in big numbers to attract bargain hunters and other shoppers.

Nothing attracts consumers more than a sign with a good promotional price.

Even if your price is not the best among the competition, a good price sign will lure all those customers who don't know the average price for that product. After all, everyone thinks that only low prices are shown on big signs, right?

Right. When consumers don't know the average price for a product, they believe the featured signs. If you put out two piles of products, one with a low price and small sign, and the other with a high price and a big sign, which pile do you think would sell out first? Try it and see.

Several retailers use the technique of lowering price by one cent to confuse the consumer. For example, instead of charging $6.00, a retailer might charge $5.99. When the price is $5.95, the effect is positive, but $5.99 seems like a cheat.

as advertised
399.99
Xbox 360 Final Fantasy XIII Special Edition
• includes games system, 2 wireless controllers, 250 GB hard drive and Final Fantasy XIII game

In this US example of attractive pricing, the retailer is better off using $399.85, even though it's a confusing number, than $399.99, which doesn't work as a gimmick anymore.

Price Tricks

When retailers try to cheat consumers by using small print or similar tricks, they might end up with a big problem. Customers who feel they've been cheated will develop a negative impression of the store that might never go away. Usually the store will lure this kind of customer one time only.

This visual trick is widely used by stores with very few sell-off items. This type of price tag is acceptable only if the store presents a large number of discounted products.

Excess of offers

You cannot afford to make mistakes when you're using big price tags. The excess paper damages the visual effect by covering the products and undercutting the benefits of the promotion. If you're charging the same price for several products, make one big tag instead of several similar ones.

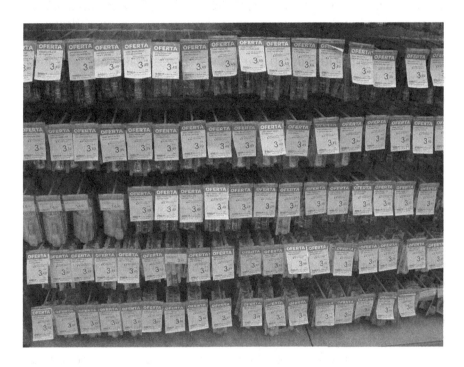

It's ridiculous to display so many price tags with the same prices, especially when they conceal the products. The correct ratio is one promotional tag per square meter of gondola.

Price Comparison

When at the same gondola we have the leading brands and others, the best strategy is to have a block of space between the cheaper brands so they are not visually close to the premium brands, because this will discourage price comparisons. The visual distance that people stop and compare prices is about 2 meters or (6 feet), 1 meter at left and 1 meter at right. After this distance there is no problem.

Position

A well-positioned product is located where the consumer would logically look for it (in the main spot of its category) or where the consumer can see it without any effort (in a promotional spot anywhere away from its category).

Main spots are established in aisles where consumers are already used to looking for a specific product. Promotional spots, on the other hand, are placed near the category, but on endcaps or in piles around the store. We notice promotional endcaps because of their good positioning in the curves as we make our way into the store. If a product is well-placed in its main spot and in some promotional spots, it will have more chances to be bought, either as a planned purchase or an impulse purchase.

Main Spot

The main spot is the place where the product is permanently allocated and the consumer is used to finding it. It is the location within the category to which the product belongs (e.g., hair color is found on the hair aisle.) Products in their main spot have spaces proportional to their participation in the market (market share) and turnover. Each product might have different market participation, depending on season. Generally speaking, products that sell more have more space than ones that sell less. Daily replenishment is usually required so that each product has the number of spaces (packaging fronts) proportional to its sales volume.

In gauging appropriate space allocation, it can be helpful to compare display size among competing products. If a product is a sales leader, it should have more space than the others.

Promotion Spot

The promotion spot is where the product is displayed for a limited time in addition to its main spot (e.g., hair color featured on the endcap of the shampoo aisle). For highest product turnover, a promotional display should always be located not far from the product's main section, in an area with a higher flow of consumers.

A promotion spot—which is almost always paid for or negotiated—should not be left in the same position and with the same signs for more than thirty days; otherwise it will no longer be an attraction. In general, sales from an extra spot begin to decrease two weeks after set-up. To refresh sales, it is recommended that retailers change the spot's location and message.

Manufacturers highly compete for endcaps, strategic product placements with good visibility. They bring featured products closer to the consumer, who gets to know them. Some are placed for years like this in the same good spot.

Never leave a product only in the promotion spot, even if the location is excellent. The habitual consumer will always look for a juice among the other juices. Think like a consumer and put the product in the most logical location for its buyers. Have you ever looked for a product in a promotional spot? Of course not. You always look for it where you think its category is, right?

Nobody looks for products in the promotion spots; consumers only find them there by chance, noticing them because of the displays and messaging. When consumers want a certain product, they will go to the appropriate aisle and try to find it.

Main spot → 88% by search
Promotion spot → 12% by chance

In most product categories, the search on the product's main spot accounts for approximately **88** percent of sales, while finding a product by chance at the promotion spot accounts for only 12 percent. Therefore every product should always be at its main spot and eventually at a promotion spot. Set up promotion spots for your product, but never abandon the product category, because this is where the consumer will try to find it.

The ideal promotional spots are ...
- visible from the door.
- well lit.
- bristling with stock.
- easy to linger in front of.
- honestly presented.
- clearly merchandised.
- well signed.
- surprising.

Remember, promotional products—those featured in promotion spots—can mean a lot of different things, such as ...
- special price offers.
- products the retailer loves and wants to showcase.
- new acquisitions.
- seasonal favorites.
- things that go together (preferably with a package price).
- new ideas.
- products in the news.
- trendy items.

A good tip for a small store is to reserve a space two meters from the front door so that customers see it the second they walk in, and to use that space to showcase a changing selection. When the space is used clearly and consistently in this way, regular and new customers alike will make it their first stop on each visit.

(Hammond, Smart Retail, *184)*

Negative Areas (Cold Spots)

The negative areas inside a store are the places where the products are not very visible. Next time you go shopping, try to notice a few of them.

Here are typical cold spots:
- At the store entrance. There is a transition area where customers entering a store have their attention on other things. In big stores, customers don't begin noticing products until they've walked about four meters inside the store.
- At the store exit (money and time have already been spent).
- At the beginning of gondolas (the first 20 cm of shelves).
- At the end of gondolas (the last 20 cm of shelves).
- Behind glass counters. (Customers will have to ask for the product, which requires effort on their part.)
- In tight aisles.
- In the four corners of the store.
- Behind pillars or close to the access doors.
- Behind tall piles or islands.
- Lower than 50 cm from the floor.
- Higher than 1.8 m from the floor.
- In areas away from the aisles' normal traffic flow.

Positive Areas (Hot Spots)

These are the areas with better visibility:
- On aisles with obligatory traffic flow.
- On wide aisles.
- On the central part of the shelves.
- On endcaps.
- In areas close to high-demand products.
- On eye-level shelves.

The Checkouts

We know that of every one hundred consumers who walk into a supermarket, fifty or so will walk through all the aisles, and twenty or so will pass by a certain product. It's difficult to come up with precise numbers, because the results depend on several conditions and vary depending on the type of store. But in general, this rule reflects how hard it is to create a whole store that is attractive, and how hard it is to lead customers to a certain section.

There's one exception to this rule: practically everyone who walks into the store will leave through the checkouts.

Checkouts are the most highly sought-after promotion spots in a retail store. These spots are negotiated with the store's main suppliers, who pay to be positioned there. That said, don't forget that checkouts are a quick passage toward the exit. If your store has this impulse products aisle before the checkouts, be careful: you should not place too many products to avoid causing visual stress to customers.

While this kind of aisle works well in supermarkets, it doesn't work that well in drugstores and convenience stores. Only impulse items work well in stores in which the rate of planned purchase is high. Stores that are geared for upper-class shoppers should avoid this type of improvised aisle, because it makes the store appear much less exclusive; such sales tactics are usually reserved for stores serving the lower-middle class.

Grouping

It is necessary to group products by category or segment in a way that's logical to consumers. Even if your suppliers' promoters want to group your products by company for their convenience, remember that consumers want to see all the options in the same product category grouped together. It's fine for all the products of the same brand to be placed together, but only as long as all those products are designed for the same general purpose.

For example, all Johnson & Johnson's women's pads can be together, as they are all feminine hygiene products. But if Johnson & Johnson diapers are placed among the pads simply because they're the same brand, the arrangement is wrong. Consumers who are looking for a specific product want to see all the options, brands, and prices together. The exception is when customers are likely to look for a product (such as makeup, perfume, or lingerie) with a predetermined brand in mind.

There are many stores that insist on mixing female and male products in the same aisle. Not only is this wrong from a logical standpoint, but it also actually discourages people from shopping for those products. In fact, in certain stores, men deserve to have exclusive spaces, because those stores carry well-defined and exclusively male lines.

Association

Association is a technique that is already standard in supermarkets and department stores, where the aisles or gondolas have planograms featuring products whose use is concomitant or related to those of the standard products in the area. Often consumers don't realize they need a product until they see it displayed with others that complement it. For example, someone buying nail polish usually will need a nail file or nail clippers or another such product. If all those products are displayed together, the retailer increases customer desire for these complementary products and the possibility of an impulse purchase.

Why is the intimate wash located close to the pads? Why is the baby oil close to the diapers? It seems logical, right? When we put shampoo close to the soaps, it is because both will be used together in the shower. Association, which is sometimes called "space management," should always be on the minds of those who create displays in gondolas or store windows. Why not expose diapers, baby oil, and baby wipes along with other baby products? Moms find it easy and practical to buy them all at once instead of walking through each aisle, collecting one thing at a time. This helps increase the average ticket and saves the customer time that can be used to shop in other sections of the store.

Cross Merchandising

Cross merchandising or cross-selling is a technique for using product association in promotion spots. When we stand in the diaper aisle and face a clip-strip display of baby ointment hanging on the shelf columns, we know we're not exactly in the baby oil section, but we're in the best promotion spot for attracting consumers who buy diapers.

A cross merchandising is an extra spot or a second position to display products that sells more than others, because the products have a link between them.

An extra spot is some product hanging out of its category. A cross merchandising is something better, because when we place a secondary location (promotional or extra spot) in a relevant category to the shopper, this complementary context makes sense.

An example: wines and liquor products on the main fixture matched by a display of chocolate. What is the logic of this? The connection here is eating something special in special moments. So this is a cross merchandising and not only an extra spot. Of course the success depends on whether the drinker is the shopper.

If on the main fixture we have cooking oil or sanitary products category, we cannot make a crossover with chocolates because it can cause a disgusting feeling and we will obtain an opposite result.

Access

Good access to products (the reach point) is essential, especially in self-service stores. A product placed too low or too high discourages customers from buying it, as they would have to ask for help. We must be very careful to place all products so they're easy to reach for people of all heights.

Heavy items must be positioned on bottom shelves to make them easier to handle. Products that are too fragile should not be placed on high shelves, or the consumer will be afraid to take them down and look at them.

Small items should be placed on higher shelves, while bigger or heavier ones should be placed on lower shelves.

Products designed for the elderly should not be placed in low places where they would have to bend over to reach them.

This backache medicine has been placed on the bottom shelves. Do you think the consumer with a backache will want to bend down to pick it up?

Children's products must be on a kid's eye level, just like candies and lollipops are at the checkout. But don't forget that the mother is the shopper, so don't place the merchandise too low. All these are positioning and access details that the retailer needs to pay attention to.

This image shows the ideal heights for adults' and children's products.

Displaying

Ever heard of the marketing concept "Visibility creates sales"? The more aggressive and lively merchandising techniques are applied in the product display areas. The well-planned product display catches consumers' attention and pushes them to buy.

On the other hand, products that aren't displayed don't sell. Many consumers aren't used to asking for an item they can't find; they will forget about it or leave it for later.

To guarantee a good display, the product needs to be …

- placed at the target customer's eye level, at a good visual angle.
- placed where the customer can reach it.
- presented in volume—that is, with a noticeable number of units.

Product visibility and accessibility are critical to POP sales.

Sight Angle and Reaching Point

Years ago, merchandisers identified the "visual comfort area" for customers perusing gondola shelves. That's the area where customers can see products without having to move their eyes or heads.

Consumers tend to look at shelves the same way they read a book: from left to right and from top to bottom.

Shoppers tend to look first at the shelves at eye level and then at the lower shelves. So display the products you hope to sell more of on the shelves located at eye level. In general, the lower a product's turnover, the lower it should be located.

Items with higher profit margins must be located not much higher than eye level and not lower than waist level.

The size of the gondolas and displays may vary according to the store, but products must be placed according to the following standards so customers can easily see and reach them:

- Maximum height to place a product is 2 m (6 ft. 5 in.).
- Eye level (best possible placement) is 1.6 m (5 ft. 2 in.).
- Hands level (where hands can reach) is 1.2–1.6 m (4 ft.–5 ft. 2 in.).
- Minimum height to place a product is 50 cm (1 ft. 6 in.). Below this height, only base or duplicate products should be stored.

According to POPAI-USA's 2014 Mass Merchant Shopper Engagement Study, due to the new habit of walking while looking at a cell phone, the standard for eye level has lowered a little, favoring hip-level shelves. Shoppers in the study tended to focus about 25 degrees below the old visual comfort area when they looked at supermarket gondolas. Their focus tended to center on the fourth shelf from the bottom.

With our increasingly frequent use of cell phones, our posture and eye direction have started to change. Regardless of the reasons for this change, it is important always to be alert to new social habits and how they can directly affect shoppers' behavior.

A shopper's visual comfort area is between the shoulders and the hands.

A promotion island shouldn't be any higher than the customer's elbow. Because most shoppers are female, it is good to limit the height of the islands so that women can see the products better.

Volume

A product displayed in great volume gives the impression of a special promotion. But even when a product is displayed in a pile, the number of units in the pile must be compatible with the turnover rate of the product when it's displayed on the shelves.

The promotional island is a display technique where great quantities of products are placed together so that the consumers can notice the product, the store's marketing, and the price.

When a product is expected to sell quickly, it is important to keep track of the number of units sold hourly from the shelf. Anticipating hourly sales can help the retailer avoid running out of the product for a day or longer.

Giving Enough Information

Shoppers usually have a fair amount of information before they even enter a store. If they don't know specific details about the product they need, they at least know the general type of product they are looking for. But when customers see a new product and don't know what it is, there's a good chance that they'll walk out of the store without getting anything, because they're afraid of buying the wrong thing. A product's packaging and store signage can offer some information, but often that's not enough.

Retailers can't assume that customers know what they are selling, including details about their products and how those products work. And many clerks talk and act as if their customers know as much as they do. Retailers should begin with the assumption every customer is completely uninformed about their products; then, after finding out the level of information a customer has, they should treat the customer accordingly.

This kind of stopper offers information that can decide the purchase.

27

Put yourself in the consumer's place when it comes to product visibility. In this picture, someone has arranged magazines in a low position that seems well exposed from a distance. But when customers get close to the display, the sight angle makes it difficult to see the various products. In this case, the display should be tilted up a bit for better reading.

CHAPTER 2:
VISUAL MERCHANDISING

Merchandising is called merchandise planning while visual merchandising is the art of implementing effective design ideas. Both have the same goal, to increase sales volume.

While merchandising is focused on the general methods, practices, and operations, visual merchandising is focused on the presentation of goods in retail outlets and emphasizes on combining visual and other sensory elements to capture attention, awaken the senses and provide the customers a wonderful buying experience to achieve more sales, which is contributory to the main goal of merchandising itself.

Merchandising has a broader sense than visual merchandising; in fact, visual merchandising is a merchandising technique which effectively uses the environment.

Visual merchandising—deciding how a store displays its merchandise—is an integral part of any successful retail operation.

Without question there is an art to attracting the shopper's eye. Visual merchandisers decide if mannequins will be used and, if so, where they should be placed; what details and accessories will be used; what signage and lighting will best highlight a product; and how store design and fixtures factor into the overall presentation. All these decisions are based on the psychology of effectively selling a specific product to a specific customer. Visual merchandisers must have good aesthetic and fashion sense combined with the ability to work in three dimensions, build props, and design department promotions.

The Rigors of Visual Merchandising

Every retailer knows that visual merchandising requires perfection, but many can't transform this knowledge into a successful strategy. The accuracy of alignment of piles, corners, rows, or any form of product grouping must be maintained at all times and with near-military precision.

Being disciplined in positioning items on shelves is not enough. It is important to plan—to establish criteria for the number of repeated pieces, a system for block definition, a logic that defines the evolution of lines, and a strategy that combines all these elements in a way that facilitates operation and replacement by the staff and selection by the consumer.

The store must constantly change, evolve, and offer customers novelties and new releases to make sure they keep coming back. The beauty of such a system is that it encourages the discovery of complementary products; the purchase of one product leads to the desire for its neighbor, which then seems equally essential in the eyes of the customer.

An excellent presentation enhances the product, while a careless display gives the impression of sloppiness, discrediting both the store and the brand.

There is not a single formula for excellent presentation; there are several. To begin with, we have a different typology for the self-service and the assisted-sale store.

A store that offers blocks of uniform and tidy product arrangement is using a self-service system, which gives an impression of plenty of product and the opportunity to make purchases with speed and agility. Retailers using a self-service system work to maintain in-store inventory; in so doing, they ration service, minimizing the need for sales staff.

But when retailers expose individualized products, selling unique pieces or small production runs, they give an impression of exclusivity. We usually associate the assisted-sale system with more prestige, better service, and higher prices. Presentation is even more important in this system; it goes beyond rigorous color selection to include a higher dose of creativity and surprise in the visual merchandising.

Creating their own systems of presentation—defining departments, lines, and products with clarity—is one of the most efficient ways retailers differentiate themselves and meet one of the greatest needs of customers: to find what they want without having to ask the seller, thus starting their decision-making process automatically. Think about it: isn't it nice to look around a store and know immediately whether or not you'll find what you need there?

(Lima, www.blogdafal.com.br)

Highlights of Basic Visual Merchandising

The objective of visual merchandising is to create a logical and visually pleasant environment that will get buyers' attention and result in increased sales. The principles of visual merchandising are easy to understand—stores should be clean and well-lit, with the merchandise displayed in segmented groups—but its most effective application is based on the merchandiser's deeper research and daily experience regarding the customer's psychology and motivation.

Here we have some important highlights:

Attract – Visual merchandising starts on the street *outside* the store. Creative, interesting window displays will draw the attention of people moving past them, making them feel engaged by the store. Many store owners make the mistake of exposing many products in window displays (to show the variety of items the store carries), but most successful window displays are selective, conveying a theme or a lifestyle or using humor to attract shoppers' curiosity. Always modify window displays according to the season, and always highlight the newest or most popular items.

Impact – You walk into a store and immediately feel like walking out. Maybe the store just wasn't as cool as it seemed, but probably something about the store or its displays displeased your eyes. The customer experience inside a store must be rich and inviting. Any prospective client should be able to walk into the store and immediately feel respected and comfortable.

Inspire – Create product displays that show customers how an item could work in their daily lives. In a clothing store, the mannequins serve that purpose; in a home decorating store, it's the nicely arranged sofa or table. In all segments of the market, customers are most likely to purchase a product when they can imagine using it.

Identify – Today, the biggest shoppers are very busy people, possibly on their way to or from work. The shoppers with less time will buy products that are easy to find, with easy-to-find price tags. Product should be organized into logical groupings, with price tags and product descriptions that are clear and easy to read.

With fierce competition in multichannel marketing and the growing need for customers' information, it's more important than ever for the retailer to differentiate himself in order to survive and excel.

A good architectonic plan and adequate space management begin with the storefront and in-store projects. Through the results of these projects, the customer senses the store's personality, quality, and level of service. The architect needs to know the store's target audience beforehand, because that information will help determine the ideal materials and finishes for the project.

A store's external architecture affects consumers' decision whether or not to enter. Seen from a distance, it forms customers' first impression. That is why the exterior project, even more than the interior, should engage and attract the target audience.

The image a store conveys through the media must be compatible with the image the store actually presents in person. Consumers should automatically associate a store's advertisements with the point of purchase; otherwise, the money spent on advertising will not be paid back in sales or brand recognition.

What makes a particular customer leave her house to go to your store? After all, she might not even know your store exists. However, maybe she likes to go for a walk or go out for a snack, meeting up with other people at the shopping mall or on the street. That's when the attractiveness of your store window comes into play. While this woman is out for a walk, something in your window grabs her attention and she decides to enter and buy.

A store can't always survive with just its loyal customers, so retailers must always be thinking about how to draw new ones.

What might catch a new customer's eye?

- novelty
- the desire to know
- the desire to experience
- beauty and aesthetics
- entertainment

And once the new customer has seen a product in the window and entered the store, she must be able to quickly find what she has seen. She must be able to touch it, feel it, try it, experience it, and interact with it. Now the product is concrete in her mind. She can visualize the experience of buying or not buying it.

This is the best chance the store has to sell. The more curiosity the window display arouses, and the more the store's internal displays continue the customer's interaction with the product, the better that chance. The buying impulse is triggered by our sight and by our desire to get something that seems great. In fact, there are entirely window-dependent product categories, especially for women: shoes, jewelry, clothes, fashion accessories, and cosmetics are the champions.

Windows

Many small retailers think it will be easy to do their own window dressing, but it is important that the job be done by a professional of visual merchandising, whose experience will pay off in sales. Retailers who don't want to pay a professional should at least take a quick visual merchandising course.

A retailer who does not know how to make a good window display and doesn't want to invest in a good window dresser should offer the job to a reputable supplier, who will set up an attractive window for free. Such an arrangement is always a good deal.

Whether the window display is simple or complex, it must be changed or refreshed as often as possible. And it must be maintained every day, because burned-out lights or a dismantled or dirty display will give the impression that the whole store is sloppy.

In order to lure consumers and make them enter the store, the window needs to tell a great story through colors, graphic elements, and lighting. Each displayed product will tell its own part of the story, depending on its shape and function. It is important that the display conveys a message that's both artistic and informational, not just showing some products, but also their prices and styles and ideas for their usage.

Windows have to be seen and assimilated from far away.

The Importance of the Window

In retail, the window is more like a door—in this case, the doorway that draws customers into a store. When customers are four meters from the front of a store, they become distracted, looking for some sign (color or logo) ahead. When they walk past the store window, they scan the door, window, and visible interior in seconds. In these two to five seconds, they reduce their pace if something interests them, or they look down and keep walking to the next window. The window is responsible for making them stop and stare and—who knows?—venture an entry.

Does the Window Sell?

A simple window sells. But an assertive, creative window with observed turnover can triple the sales of a regular window. Some American clothing stores have a serious attitude regarding their windows: they set a window and observe the effect on passersby for three hours. If nobody stops to look, they disassemble everything and start over until it works.

In the case of clothing stores or boutiques, windows are extremely important, since they are the major vehicles for attracting customers inside a store. The window display is even more important for small retailers who do not advertise, because it is their main instrument for attracting sales. In this case, evaluating the performance of a window display is indispensable. Modern retailers know that the well-displayed merchandise is the most requested by customers; display windows are just as important as advertising and promotion.

Window Life Span

Each window must change according to the type of product and business: in fashion, every day; in electronics, every week. It all depends on the customer interest generated daily. In order to gauge the interest turnover of each of the exposed products, just notice whether someone asks for it. A fashion product that does not succeed in two days should swap places with another product or leave the window. If it does succeed, keep it in the featured place until the stock runs low.

Planning

Always plan a window in advance. Planning a sequential monthly or semimonthly theme is essential to giving the store a consistent image. The whole annual promotional calendar must be outlined ahead of time so the ideas can flow until the day of assembly. Put down on paper or on screen all aesthetic and conceptual aspects of the design, including the materials you plan to use, the time it will take to gather and prepare the elements, and the money available to spend on your display.

Planning for a window display must be based on four evaluations:
1. analysis of products to be exposed (size / color / shape / groups / quantity)
2. analysis of customer profiles and preferences (price / gender / usage / search)
3. creation of message to the observer (signs / directions / inferences / comprehension)
4. the store's focus on and identification of the target audience

Kinds of Products and Their Windows

For each segment or product, there is a window pattern. The size of the product is the first consideration. An outfit can be admired from two to three meters away; jewelry can't. To admire a ring, you practically have to press your face into the glass. That shows that jewelry must be at eye level and well lit. Clothes, on the other hand, should be on mannequins, with their chests at customers' eye level. Obviously, the positioning is very different.

An electronics window must be kinetic, with movement and images. Everything must be turned on and suggesting its use. Children's stores must attract mothers and kids; the height of the products should be lower than one meter, and the display should feature bright colors and characters. Even a very busy window, displaying many different products, should be planned according to the type of product or customer. That will make the display more easily understood by anyone who sees it.

Elements of Composition and Attractiveness

1. Never fill up a window, and never leave a window empty (implying that there is no stock).
2. Create a tasteful arrangement so that all the pieces work in harmony. A window is a composition, a work of art, all the pieces should complement each other.
3. Your composition should have a central line and be well balanced.
4. Do not make a window with all the products in the same color, even if it's the trendiest fashion color. Remember that there will always be people who dislike that color, so show them that you have an assorted selection.

5. Don't forget to put price tags on every product. Most people won't enter a store if they notice that prices in the display window are hidden.
6. The product is the star of the display, not the decorations or background. You're not selling either of them, right? They're just part of the composition and shouldn't overshadow the products.

The Power of Lighting

Dim lighting keeps customers away. Unbalanced lighting does not lead customers to where we want them to look or to go, and in fact it may distract them from the focal or promotional spot. Sufficient, well-directed lighting creates an attractive stage. A good window dresser can use lighting to create amazing effects that will draw people's eye to the products. Lighting is also very important inside a store. A dark interior may jeopardize sales, even if the windows are brightly illuminated. Leave both areas well lit so as not to scare customers away.

Final Exam

During and after the display assembly, observe the results from outside. During assembly, especially, visually examine how the set piece works together (e.g., height, length, alignment, proportions, lighting, focal points, composition axis, visibility of prices) without being too stuck to the original design. Adjustments will always be needed to finalize the window.

The Perfect Window

The perfect window is one that grabs people's attention in a single, distracted glance; draw them in with the products; helps them decide whether to go inside by including pricing information; and remains etched in the minds of consumers who, for whatever reason, decide not to go inside today, but who will come back tomorrow to shop.

Sale Windows

Never completely close your store window during a sale. While a closed window might not be a problem for your current customers, a sales period is the best time for someone who isn't a customer to make an impulsive decision to enter. Discounted prices might be what pulls in this shopper and wins you a customer. So sales are your chance to gain new customers—if, of course, you show what is on sale.

If your window is closed, anyone who doesn't know your store will keep walking without knowing what you sell, not to mention what's on sale. So by all means shout, "Sale!"—but show what you sell, please!

If I am not a regular customer at this store, how can I know what it sells?

Certain types of retail stores are very window dependent. Such is the case with shoe stores, which are obliged to show almost their whole stock. These retailers need spacious windows so the display doesn't look cluttered and sloppy, an effect that can devalue the products.

Ambiance

A store's exterior and window displays have the task of attracting consumers to the store. In turn, the internal ambiance informs and seduces predisposed consumers, acclimating them to buy.

Cows evoke thoughts of a farm, where all products are fresh.

There are two types of ambiance: promotional and institutional.

The promotional atmosphere is aimed only at increasing turnover of a product or an entire category. Retailers use this scenographic atmosphere to break down consumer resistance toward any fragile category like dairy products, seafood, meat, etc. As consumers of these products tend to be particularly wary of poor quality, some retailers create an atmosphere referencing the farm or the sea, for example, which makes the consumer subconsciously imagine the place of the product's origin, where everything is fresh.

The institutional atmosphere is designed to create a certain mood and appeal to customers' sense of nostalgia or patriotism. Displays that reference Christmas, Carnival, Thanksgiving, or historical events benefit to the store while not relating to any product directly. Such seasonal décor is highly positive; it captivates the customers, who perceive the place as more beautiful and pleasant and less overtly commercial.

Retailers must experiment with their displays, changing them around and analyzing which displays work best for certain audiences and products.

Purchasing Atmosphere

What is the Purchasing Experience?

The purchasing experience is the entire path that the consumer takes: observing the storefront, deciding to enter, parking the car, taking the first few steps inside the store, dealing with the employees, touring the store, seeing the merchandise, waiting in line, and checking out, all along the way making observations about time, smell, sound, quality, and service.

The purchasing experience and atmosphere are what form an indelible image of the store in a consumer's mind. It is that image that will make the consumer either shop there again or never return.

What Composes a Good Atmosphere?

The term *shopping atmosphere*, despite its abstract sound, is actually a quite tangible quality when it comes to visual merchandising. The term refers to several elements of the store environment—the visual cues, lighting, colors, music, and aromas chosen to stimulate customers' perceptions and emotional responses, which, in the end, may affect their buying decisions.

The characteristics of a store—the position of products, the number and height of counters and gondolas, the floor, the walls, the ceiling, the air temperature, even the people walking around the store—all affect whether the consumer feels tempted to buy.

Every element that goes into displaying a product is manipulated in order to generate greater sales.

Knowing What In-Store Atmosphere to Use

There are five basic elements to pleasing consumers.
Put yourself in their place and check the following:
* how consumers "see" the POP (decor/visibility)
* how consumers feel inside the POP (comfort/facilities)
* how well employees attend to consumers (warmth and competence of employees)
* how well products meet consumers' expectations (location/quality/prices)
* how consumers ultimately perceive the store, whether or not they make a purchase

If you do not want to actually research these questions, try to notice customers' facial expressions. Do they seem satisfied or dissatisfied? Calm or hurried? Confident or unsure?

Consumers always evaluate the point of purchase and the products together; it is very important that they feel comfortable inside a store so that they will remain faithful to it. You've probably seen it for yourself: in a pleasant, convenient shopping environment, you tend to lose track of time and get more pleasure out of buying.

How to Create a Buying Atmosphere

Here are just some of the factors that can influence customers' buying decisions at purchasing time:

- storefront, exterior illumination, windows, architecture
- background music, sound
- characteristic perfume or aromas
- interior lighting, colors
- decorations, plants
- orientation of each section
- promotional piles or offers
- posters, signage
- merchandise displays
- amount of walking space
- air conditioning
- employee uniforms
- variety of products
- easy parking, drive-through window
- restrooms, changing facilities, chairs, rest areas
- employees' friendliness and customer care
- manager's or owner's friendliness and customer care

Keeping in mind the variations among points of purchase, because each store has a different project and design, retailers should be aware of what the research says about what's important in the preparation of a pleasing retail environment. The chart below indicates that consumers are governed primarily by vision.

The Human Perception According to Senses:

Taste: 1 %
Touch: 1.5 %
Smell: 3.5 %
Hearing: 11 %
Sight: 83 %

(Veronis, Shler & Associates)

The Buying Experience and the Five Senses

All consumers are vulnerable to making an impulse purchase, but they need to be properly stimulated in order to do so. Pedro L. Roccato says on his website DirectChannel.com that when we visit a store, we are seeking an individual purchasing experience. Many times, our decision whether or not to buy something isn't based on whether we really need the product or service or even on how much we are willing to pay; instead it depends on our particular state of mind at the moment of purchase.

For how long do retailers observe the buying experience of their customers?

How many retailers pay attention to and respond to changes in their customer profile? Retailers cannot forget that they are the administrators of their customers' perception at the point of purchase. Today, paying attention to consumers' sensory perception at the POP is very important to retail businesses. Stores must use great lighting; offer products that are well displayed and organized in sections for easy location; stock a variety of products that are suitable for customers who frequent the POP; incorporate ambient sound and scent; and offer consistent support from a team of well-trained salespeople who are attentive to the real needs of their customers.

Some stores have already paid attention to these elements and are managing to stand out among their competitors. One of the resources stores now use is gauging the effectiveness of their window displays at different times by profiling the customers who circulate in front of the store at certain moments. This is an example of individualization. The standardization of visual merchandising in retail is an insult to individualization. With the constant retractions in the retail market in recent years, it's clear that retailers need to reinvent their businesses every day. Consumers are always thirsting for novelty and new experiences. By being attentive to their needs, retailers can generate increasingly positive results for their businesses.

Sight

The color combinations used in stores must attract the target audience and highlight specific products. For large stores, the important elements are uncluttered walls, white ceilings to save light, and décor that complements the store's informative elements. Some stores may be more daring. An example is Sephora, which uses black furniture and dramatic illumination to create a unique atmosphere.

Lighting should guide the shopper through the store; it must produce a pleasant skin tone where there are mirrors; it must be appropriately scaled in booths or testers; it must provide sufficient clarity for the employees to perform their tasks; and it should highlight the best areas of the store. A lighting plan can suggest either exclusivity, privacy, and personalized customer care or self-service, convenience, and relaxation.

Although there is no scientific proof, some researchers have stated that lighting changes the mood and behavior of consumers. The quantity of light stimulates the eyes to blink more or less, either invigorating or numbing the senses.

Good lighting is responsible for illuminating the environment, highlighting merchandise, decorating special spaces, and complementing the style and personality of the store. In addition to conveying a sense of cleanliness, well-lit environments are pleasant and therefore attractive to the consumer. The lighting design should be adjusted so that the store does not have too much or too little light. Dark stores, or those that scrimp on lighting to save energy, create a very unappealing atmosphere that discourages customers from entering. If a store appears to be unlit when seen from the street during the day, that's a sign of poor lighting. Every store should be lit, even during the day.

The type of lighting also needs to be chosen with care, so as to not modify the colors of the products. In the windows, spotlights can be used to emphasize the merchandise, enhancing certain products and attracting the customer's eye.

Hearing

Music can be vital to a store's ambiance. Like color and lighting, it can improve or denigrate the general atmosphere of the store. Music is an element that can easily be changed or adjusted according to the season or occasion simply by changing the song selection.

In general, avoid using commercial radio stations. Currently, retailers use different types of music to stimulate consumer behavior in different ways at different times. It may sound strange, but the rhythm of music can even help control the flow of shoppers in large stores.

The most effective playlist often includes calm, soothing music, mostly acoustic or classical melodies. A common error is for employees to put on songs that they enjoy. When employees control the music, they tend to get distracted, crank up the volume, or choose songs of dubious tastefulness. When a store has customers older than their forties but it plays heavy metal, its customers will get irritated and end up leaving sooner, resulting in decreased sales. Light, slow music predisposes customers to forget the time and buy more products.

Smell

The majority of purchasing decisions in a store are based on need or emotion. After vision—the sense that introduces us to products—smell is the sense that evokes the most emotions. A particular scent gives personality to the environment and evokes memories, desires, and feelings like hunger, sorrow, regret, and even happiness.

Today there are companies that can develop any kind of smell or fragrance to be used in magazine advertisements or stores to awaken consumers' desire for a specific product. With products like perfumes, cosmetics, toiletries, diapers, and soaps, this strategy usually increases regular sales by more than 20 percent. Notice how consumers choose soap or diapers in a store: usually they smell the product to make sure they like the scent. They will purchase the product only if they are pleased.

Many retailers try to use fragrances in their stores to create a certain personality. They believe that some fragrances encourage customers to linger and buy more products. Before a retailer uses one aroma for the whole store, however, it's important to plan and test well to make sure that the scent is attractive to everyone, without exceptions.

Research conducted by Professor Eric R. Spangenberg of Washington State University showed that customers in perfumed environments perceive time as being shorter than it really is. Such a perception is beneficial to the retailer when the shopper is selecting merchandise as well as waiting in a queue. A perfumed retail environment also gave customers a greater sense of well-being than did a nonperfumed store.

Taste

The best way to sell a product is to display it and put it in customer's hands. But, many stores sell hidden products, behind counters, expecting people to find them. Glass counters and windows were invented to show products, and show them beautifully. The displays in bakeries and pastry shops are the best examples of the value of a display. We stock our eyes in pastry products because of the taste we can imagine immediately. Our eyes decide what to buy, and the taste will decide to come back or not.

Make your customers hungry—make them eat with their eyes!

Touch

It is said that putting a product in the consumer's hand is 50 percent of the sale. Let the customer try, feel, and hold the product. There are still stores that enclose and isolate products so they won't be ruined. Would you buy a couch or a mattress without sitting on it first?

Let customers feel your product. Put the product in their hands, or let them try it out. Allowing customers to touch a product is the easiest way to make a connection with them and make the sale.

> **Put the product in customers' hands so they can see, touch, feel, test ... and buy.**

Color Sensations

Colors evoke certain sensations that affect customer behavior. They can make a customer loyal for life or make that customer want to escape.

Color is a visual feeling that involves objects, a source of light, and the eyes and brain of an observer. After being captured by the eyes and interpreted by the brain, color is processed individually according to factors, such as the physical condition of the observer. The eyes capture the colors and light and send impulses to the brain, which influences the consumer's reaction. The color can cause sensations of heat or cold, numbness or effervescence, indifference or attraction. Customers' reaction to color is also influenced by personal tastes and regional and cultural differences (e.g., red carries a different meaning in England than in China). Color quickly attracts the eyes, drawing consumers' attention here or there. Customers who are drawn to a product because of a color react immediately, either liking it and feeling pleasure or disliking it and looking away.

Discerning the preferences of the target consumer enables a retailer to be assertive in its choice of colors in packaging, advertising campaigns, and store design. A store can either succeed or go bankrupt because of a color that is poorly chosen or used. A store that is pleasing to the eye initiates shoppers' desire to enter, while an unpleasant (dark or strange) color diverts customers, making them walk away.

Both bright colors and pastels are pleasing to the majority of people. Dark or "hot" colors enhance specific types of products if they relate to your consumption environment, for example: drinks, romance, and strength. People decide to buy and carry the proposed idea in the package, its design and its colors.

The Brazilian designer Gilberto Strunck says that all manufacturers and retailers should understand the importance of colors to rapid identification of their brands. "A well planned retail is one that leads to the extreme art of persuasion, presenting products and services in scenarios so seductive that it becomes virtually impossible for people to not buy something in the store," he says.

Strunck believes that using light colors in a store visually extends the retail space, but a store that is totally white can seem too cold. By the same taken, dark colors make very large environments more cozy and welcoming. Pastel shades are calm and not recommended for the more popular retail stores. Strong colors should be used for detail only; they draw attention but can be tiring if used too much. "The predominant color on the inside of a retail organization has a direct relationship with the understanding of the personality of your brand and should be chosen with the aim of serving as a support for the exhibitors of products and services that will be sold. Color is an emotional communication related to culture," he says.

In the dark, red turns brown and gray turns black. Without light, color dies; therefore a store and its products need to be well lit. A store that isn't will frighten the clientele. There are customers who are afraid to go into a dark store.

("*Cor e sua influência na farmácia*")

Light

In fact, what customers see is not an object itself, but the light that hits its surface. So getting a good result from using color in the POP depends on the lighting, including the amount of natural light. As a room gets dark, the colors of the objects inside start transforming into various shades of gray. For this reason, the type of lighting used in a store directly affects how customers visualize the store's environment and merchandise.

Different types of bulbs—incandescent, fluorescent, halogen, dichroic, and LED, among others—emit different kinds of light that result in distinct color temperatures. Fluorescent bulbs are cool. They make skin tones, cosmetics, and objects less attractive, with an effect quite different from that of sunlight. Incandescent bulbs are warm, with more attractive results. There are dozens of lighting options for retail; many retailers combine various sources of light. The desired atmosphere, the initial cost of the equipment, and the cost of use over time are some of the factors to be considered in a lighting design project. The important thing is that the result as a scenographic environment reflects the personality of the retail brand, highlighting in special way the merchandise for sale.

The contrast between light and dark can stop sales in some parts of a store. See this black wall with black merchandise on it? Our eyes go to the light and forget the rest.

How Can I Use This Knowledge in My Store?

To start, simply realize that all human senses – vision, hearing, smell, taste and touch – are considered as the ambience. Regarding the vision, for example, it is known that 83% of human perception is visual. Therefore, the ambient lighting, the colors and the composition of non-polluted visuals of the POP are essential. The hearing of customer is easily reached with the selection of a gentle and serene music; in a tone enough to be heard and that it does not harm the conversation. The touch may be activated by means of differentiated floors between the sections and the continuous products touch. The climate of the store also contributes to comfort. For the taste, the store can use some products that can be tasted in the store during its launch, or can also simply offer a tea or coffee, as several stores do.

Design Project

In the design or reformulation process, it is of greatest importance to hire skilled professionals with experience in commercial spaces. That means hiring an architect, at the very least. A retailer who presumes to know how to do everything, without help, generally ends up with a poorly designed, dysfunctional, or even unappealing space. The choice of good service providers in a store's preoperational phase is as critical as the choice of suppliers with whom the store will work after its launch.

For the hired professionals to do their best work, it is absolutely essential that retailers precisely explain their positions and visions; otherwise, the resulting projects will not reflect the identities the retailers had hoped to convey. Planning and building stores with a big impact is a strategic task for retailers who want to stand out by offering consumers a consistent experience.

Consumers are more informed, demanding, and sophisticated than ever, and competition from online retail has forced traditional stores to be unique and more attractive. Despite the growth and convenience of electronic formats, however, the customer experience will always be much richer in a physical store.

Store Planning

Professional store planners study psychology, ergonomics, and anthropometry in order to work with visual merchandising to tailor retail projects according to consumers' characteristics.

From the aesthetic point of view, effective visual merchandising creates a favorable and memorable impression, simplifies the process of buying, induces the consumer to buy more and return again, facilitates the work of the sellers, and makes the store a fun and exciting place in which to shop and work.

From the technical point of view, effective visual merchandising raises the productivity of stores, turns the stock, increases sales per square meter, makes sales more profitable, increases the average ticket, and reduces the need for markdowns and sales.

Visual Design is as Important as Price

An efficient architectural design should be discreet, giving visibility to the merchandise and contributing to the positive buying experience. In the opinion of editor Felipe Zmoginski, there is no doubt that the visual design of a store is just as important as price, packaging, advertising, customer relationship, and service. Good ambiance in retail boosts sales, makes it easier for customers to shop, and creates loyal customers. Efficient communication with customers is also very important, because it helps the retailer become part of the community in which it operates. Analyzing the performance of the competition is also critical.

It is ideal for retailers to promote their strengths through traditional means or technological communication (e.g., media advertisements, promotional material, brochures, banners, etc.). Even small retailers can find a way to engage in effective communication that results in a good store image and generates a return on the investment.

The point of purchase offers a unique way to communicate with customers. Knowing how to "talk with them" is fundamental to improving sales.

Every environment has a peculiar way of communicating with consumers. A church, for example, is not just a place to pray and attend religious services. It has a certain architecture and imagery that encourages reflection and introspection. In the same way, an amusement park simulates favorable conditions for exploring the senses, with strong colors and music and attractions filled with movement and sound.

Until recently, these standard concepts were foreign to retail, which left the ambiance inside a store up to the discretion of the manager or owner. There was no well-defined, organic methodology about how aesthetics could impact a store's bottom line.

But the increased competition in retail—including the convenience of remote shopping via the Internet—has forced POPs to evaluate new aspects of retail operations, including the store layout. It is in this context of innovation—between the search for wider profit margins and the consequent increase in the average ticket—that experts, academics, and executives have started to pay more attention to research in the areas of merchandising and layout. At the forefront of this segment are the supermarkets. Well attuned to global retail trends and good billing, the big network wholesalers have invested in research and market analysis and noticed the direct influence that a store's environment can have on sales.

Studies conducted by the Fundação Instituto de Administração (FIA) reveal, for example, that a more comfortable environment makes consumers spend more time in the store, and that this time is fundamental to their decisions whether or not to buy a product.

Many experts believe the solution is to use in your favor the eight languages spoken in the modern retail store: oral, climatic, gustatory, visual, sound, signage, aromatic, and proxemics.

Oral

Don't Stress Your Customer

This language is directly linked to human contact between customers and attendants. Store staff should adopt an appropriate use of language and tone of voice when they speak to customers. In an esoteric store, for example, they need to speak in low tones. It is always necessary to use a clear and objective vocabulary and avoid simplified terms that reveal unpreparedness or ignorance about the products.

A common mistake is for retailers to train attendants to use standardized or stereotypical speech. Sentences like "Thanks for waiting," "Just a moment, sir," or "Can I help you?" should be used very few times. Repeated use of these questions or phrases, as well as expressions used by telemarketers, irritates consumers, increasing their desire to buy only what they need quickly so they can leave. The result is a decrease in the average ticket.

A common cause of stress to consumers is when they suspect an employee is trying to sell them something rather than help them. Even worse is when consumers suspect that an employee knows less about the product than they do. Thus it is necessary for retailers to train their sales staff not only about the products and the market but also about dealing with customers in a positive, unintimidating way. Oral communications between employees and customers should serve as invitations for customers to stay in the store, even if the shoppers do not say this literally.

Climatic

The Location Must Be Pleasant

Who hasn't left a store without buying some necessity because the place was too hot or too cold? When faced with an uncomfortable in-store climate, a customer's first reaction is to get out of the place as soon as possible. In this case, it is worth using common sense and setting the temperature in your favor. Another bit of advice from the experts: listen to your customers. Pay attention when someone says that the place is too hot or too cold, and act quickly to correct the problem.

Gustatory

Give Pleasure to the Consumer

If your store can offer samples for tasting, don't miss the opportunity to do so. It is a pleasure that you give to your consumer while saying implicitly, "This pleasure can be purchased here."

Visual

Chromatic Communication

Who hasn't heard that all the fast-food restaurants decorate with red in order to arouse the appetite while annoying the vision, inducing customers to buy something and then leave the place as soon as possible? The idea is to force turnover. Visual communication is one area of merchandising in which common sense isn't always useful; retailers should enlist the help of a specialist.

Sound

Use Music to Generate Tranquility and Identification

The exploitation of music is still nascent in retail. Some supermarkets are using sounds of the sea in the fish area, and sports stores play electronics hits at a low volume. The idea is to create thematic unity and awaken the consumer through sound. In some store segments, there are music channels with soothing sounds, such as instrumental music, designed to entertain the customer and create a feeling of comfort. Other stores insert commercials in their sound programming to announce special promotions. If this technique is not overdone, it is an interesting alternative. The experts' advice, however, is to test various alternatives and evaluate the results.

Aromatic

The Sense of Smell Awakens Desires

Fast-food restaurants are said to allow the smell of their food to linger in the air on purpose; by doing so, they're hoping to win customers who pass by their stores. But sophisticated restaurants avoid excessive smell. The reasons for the differing strategies are obvious. Fast-food stores want turnover: they want people to eat and leave. The restaurant wants a higher ticket and, better yet, they want customers to stay longer, enjoying the experience of a dinner along with their favorite drink and perhaps dessert. In a store, the ideal aroma is the one that conveys a sense of freshness and cleanliness.

Signage

Inform the Consumer

As the name implies, signage is the messaging conveyed by signs displayed in-store. A successful signage project communicates information to customers in a clear way—the store logo, the forms of payment accepted, a store map, prices, hours of operation, etc. The idea is to show the consumer visually all the information they need to feel comfortable making a purchase.

Proxemics

Freedom to Walk

The proxemic function is the relationship between consumers and the space they occupy. An aisle with large fronts of products creates a feeling of unity and dimensionality (which may or may not be desirable). In the case of retail stores, the general recommendation is that the customer should have more space to circulate among the products—a feeling of freedom, in other words.

Another aspect to be studied in the proxemic function is cross merchandising or cross-selling, the displaying of related elements according to the target consumer in a particular place. Cross-selling is planned based on the crossing of sales data: people who buy diapers also buy diet juices; customers who buy shampoos buy more deodorant, etc.

Shelving also should be arranged to allow for the best proxemic function. A variable that is intrinsic to the quality of customer service is the type of fixtures a retailer uses. Shelves must not be too wide or too deep, especially in small stores. They also should not be too high, or the store will lose its sense of spaciousness. The fixtures used at the checkout and customer service counters also have to be planned to encourage freedom of movement.

(Zmoginski, "A Partitura do Varejo", 36)

Always put yourself in the consumer's place.
Imagine yourself shopping in your store.

CHAPTER 3:
THE STORE

No matter what consumers buy, they expect the purchase to fulfill some human need, physical or emotional. The act of purchasing creates an emotional bond between the consumer and the store. But customer loyalty to a particular product or brand is not perennial. Depending on the product, its quality, its price, and its benefits, customers can migrate very easily to a different product. The relationship between the consumer and the product is a one-way street: the product does not interact with the consumer.

But the relationship between a consumer and a store is different. In this case, we are talking about a relationship between people, an interaction that is completed by the ambiance of the store. The loyalty of consumers to a product depends on the manufacturer rather than the retailer. The loyalty of consumers to the store, however, depends exclusively on the retailer.

Here are the most important points a retailer should remember when developing a store's image:
- The store name should be short; easy to read, pronounce, and remember; and capable of suggesting the images and feelings that the retailer wants to instill in the consumer.
- The store logo should be visually powerful, simple, easy to see, and consistent with the products the store sells.
- The storefront should have architecture that complements the store's identity, have a highly visible sign, and feature windows with the products facing out to catch the interest of potential customers.
- The store should have an inviting entry without obstacles or guards. Most retail stores have attractive entries that give a glimpse of their bright interiors. In the few seconds while consumers are passing the door, their attention is diverted from the outside to the inside of the store, making them decide whether or not to enter.

Location

The location of a retail store can make it or break it. Socioeconomic and demographic factors, competitor activity, and market saturation all have an impact on retail sales. In order to choose the best location, retailers need access to this essential information.

The methodology behind site selection is not just a matter of choosing between a street store and a shopping center. Research has shown that certain stores do better in very specific circumstances, and knowledge of that research should be applied to ensure that a store is located in the best possible position. Here are the three key items to consider before you decide on a retail site:

1. Macroeconomics and Demographics

What are the economic trends at play in the retail sector in general, and what's the broad economic profile of the area you're considering? It's always worth staying on top of retail sector research, as those statistics will be essential to your decision.

What is the demographic profile of the community? Don't just think about what's there now; think about how the area could change over the years and the opportunities and challenges that change might present.

2. The Middle-Macro Mindset

Shopping center or street store? This question is all about the potential footfall from existing shoppers in the area, so it's time to take a closer look at the surroundings. What other stores are close by, and more important, what mindset will shoppers have when they're in the area? Are the surrounding shops larger retail chains or smaller independents, and what does the answer mean for your success?

Being surrounded by retailers that complement your products will increase your chances of footfall. On the other hand, if the shopping mall or street stores are more fashion focused, even if there are thousands of potential customers per day, they aren't likely to be in the right frame of mind to buy electronics. A fashion accessories store, for example, would have much more success there.

3. Micro Matters

Yes, the micro details matter. Take a shopping mall, for example: What level would your store be on? How close would it be to the entrance? Is the center's architecture linear or curved? All these factors will have an impact on how many people will pass by or walk into your store.

For example, in a curved shopping center, more people will tend to walk on the inside, not the outside, of a curve. While the shoppers themselves may not even realize they do this, there is a pattern to how they walk around and shop. A difference of ten meters can make a huge difference to the number of customers your store attracts. Have conversations with existing retailers in the area and learn from their experience. Try spending a few hours studying the shoppers in the area; notice how the traffic pattern changes at different times of the day and on different days of the week.

There are many factors retailers should consider before choosing a store location. From traffic analysis to zoning requirements, there is a lot of data to examine before deciding on the perfect spot.

In theory, there are no "bad" shopping centers—just retailers who haven't done their analysis and research.

Details

Before choosing a store location, define how you imagine your business.
- What do your customers look like?
- What do you want to sell?
- Are you selling something you like or something people need in this particular area?
- How much retail space do you need?

The money you have to invest in a new store will not always be enough to cover feasibility and location studies. But there are companies that specialize in developing these reports according to your market and demand. If you do not want risk your investment, or if you feel insecure about your choices, look for a consultant or one of those companies.

Before you rent or buy a space, it's important that you ...
- get preliminary potential studies.
- identify the market potential.
- get a preliminary evaluation of the kind of enterprise to be built at the chosen site.
- define areas of influence around the store (mall, hospital, school).
- collect data on main competitors.
- get geographical visualization of traffic generator poles.
- quantify your target audience.
- estimate the potential for the product or service categories in your business.
- study side traffic and direction.
- analyze a similar or very different neighborhood.

Traffic and Parking

Don't confuse a lot of traffic with a lot of customers. Major streets are not good places to open a store if drivers cannot easily see it or stop. Retailers want to be located where there are many shoppers, but only if those shoppers meet the definition of their target market. Except in places without car access, you should have space for parking, ease of access, convenience, and safe walkways for pedestrians.

Before you rent a store, check the following:
- How many people walk or drive past the proposed location?
- Is the area served by public transportation?
- Can customers and delivery trucks get in and out of the parking lot easily?
- Is there adequate parking?

Visibility

The more visibility your retail store has, the less advertising you'll need. An attractive exterior will reinforce the memory of your store in the minds of consumers who see it. When considering visibility, look at the location from the customer's point of view.

Can the store be seen from the main flow of traffic? Will your sign be easily seen? If you were to stand on the sidewalk on either side of the store, would you be able to see the front? If you were to approach the store by car, would you be able to see it a block away? Would anybody understand what the store is about from a block away, on foot or by car? Contact the proper local authorities about signage regulations.

Compatibility with the Area

Before signing a lease, be sure you understand all the rules, policies, and procedures related to your retail store location. Ask about any restrictions that may affect your retail operation and any future city planning that could change traffic or zoning. It is important to make your store compatible with other buildings in the neighborhood in terms of size, architecture and style.

Neighborhood and Competition

The other businesses in your prospective location can help or hurt your retail shop. Determine if the types of businesses nearby are compatible with your store. For example, a high-end fashion boutique may not be successful next to a discount variety store. By the same token, your boutique can't be near a vehicle repair center or gas station, because most women don't like to frequent those places. Place your boutique next to a nail or hair salon, and it will probably do much more business.

Rent and Extra Costs

Besides the base rent, consider all the potential costs involved when choosing a retail store location.

- Who pays for lawn care, building maintenance, utilities, and security?
- Who pays for the upkeep and repair of the heating and air units?
- Will you need to make any repairs (painting or remodeling) to fit your needs?
- Will the retailer be responsible for property taxes?

The location you can afford now and the one you can afford in the future should vary. It is difficult to create sales projections for a new business, but one way to help determine how much rent you can pay is to find out what sales similar retail businesses are making and how much rent they're paying.

Don't feel rushed into making a decision about where to put your retail store. Take your time, research the area, and have patience. If you have to change your schedule and push back the date of the store's opening, then do so. Waiting to find the perfect location is far better than just settling for the first place that comes along. The wrong location could ruin your retail business.

Store Floor Plan

The store floor plan includes the positions of the fixtures (gondolas, checkouts, sections, etc.) necessary to operate the store and control the flow of consumers. The best plan balances several goals:

- Consumers should be able to move easily among the fixtures. Ample space between gondolas encourages consumers to spend more time in the store and buy more than what they had planned, and it stimulates flow in the aisles.
- There should be good space in front of the counters for customer service.
- There should be enough space to highlight and promote products.
- Categories should be separated in a logical way that facilitates self-service shopping.

The preliminary layout plan must take into account the type of consumer you want to attract, in addition to the products you want to sell.

Even though layout experts always strive to do their best, there are always some areas of a store that are more lucrative than others. When positioning a popular product or promotion within a store, try to choose areas that sell more and have a greater flow of consumers; don't waste lucrative space on products that don't sell well.

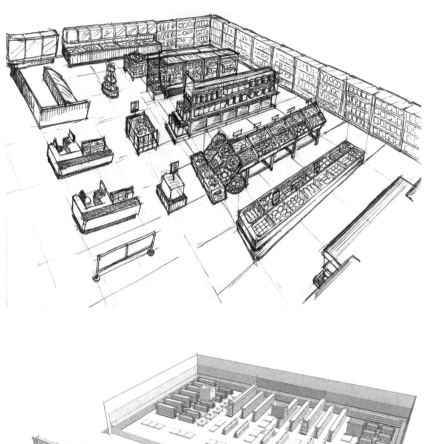

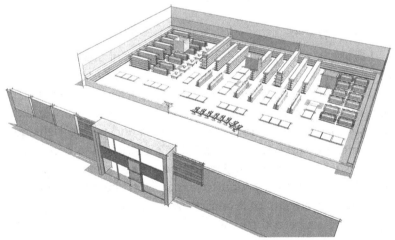

Top: a preliminary layout plan for a small store.
Bottom: a layout study for a medium store.

Layout design from Novarejo (Novarejo.com.br).

Retailers can use multiple locations within a store to expose merchandise:

- gondolas and shelves
- big baskets
- simple piles (stacks of one type of product)
- multiple piles (stacks with two or more products)
- island (big, isolated pile in the middle of a wide aisle)
- endcaps (always with signs and pallet covers)
- a pile against a wall
- displays (for product dispensers or a product promotion)
- stands (assembled in a special space or corner)
- counters
- windows (external or internal)
- checkouts
- outside, at sidewalk

Basic merchandising is easy, but it must be done with great care and detail in all parts of the store so that shoppers can get familiar with its brands, products, and services. Then they will become faithful customers who will lead the business to success.

Store Layout

Layout is a project, a design. A successful store project is one that maximizes profits and returns the investment in the area.

The traditional method of conducting a layout project is for the retailer to think about the store design with the aim of exposing the merchandise on the correct shelves and in the right quantity and varieties, with visual impact that is suitable and comfortable to the consumer. Strong competition between retailers, however, has forced stores of every kind to expand on the traditional concept and embrace layouts that encourage the consumer to spend more time in the store and to have contact and an experience with the displayed products, with the goal of increasing sales.

At a time when retailers are already battling for a competitive edge based on products, price, location, and promotion, the point of purchase itself has become a place to gain an edge.

Shopping nowadays is not always a pleasure. With so many retail options, including online retail, it takes more than a good commodity to make consumers leave home and choose a specific store. Therefore it is more necessary than ever to create a differentiated and pleasant design to promote visits and sales. A store is like a theater stage, where walls, ceiling, floor, equipment, windows, and communications all support the main cast—the products. So when hiring a professional to draw the layout of your store, don't just look for an ordinary architect; find an experienced retail architect.

In addition to having a layout that can scale up the productivity of the space, the store design should suit the store's location, target audience, and style. The ambiance and atmosphere of the site need to positively influence the decisions of the store's customers.

The layout of a store should include the following elements:
- specialized fixtures (the narrowest possible)
- moving shelves, pegboards, and other product spaces appropriate to category type
- promotional areas for extra spots, endcaps and so on
- equipment for promotions (wheeled for easy replacement)
- groupings by category and family of use
- linear displays of product families and subfamilies
- external and internal windows and their access points
- areas of movement for employees and consumers
- support area / small office and delivery area
- service door / area for deposits/loading and unloading areas
- rest areas and bathrooms
- parking spaces
- displays and exclusive spaces for brands

In addition, implementation of the layout should consider:
- services organization, product presentation, position of checkouts, and packaging
- customer care / exchanges / security
- illumination between gondolas (targeting the products and the aisles)
- floor surfaces (neither slippery nor abrasive)
- small equipment with wheels for easy handling

This 3-D preliminary study of a store layout shows all the store's sections and their predicted circulation. Layout design from Novarejo (Novarejo.com.br).

Deciding where to put each section within the layout is not a difficult task, but it requires logic and planning. The objective is to anticipate the needs of the consumer touring the store. All the products should be grouped into departments, each of which will work best in certain areas of the store. These departments can be classified as fixed, seasonal, impulse, high-margin, low-margin, and high-theft. (This last department should be in a place where the employees can see it.) A well-planned store layout allows a retailer to maximize sales for each square foot of allocated selling space within a store.

Store layouts generally show the size and location of each department, any permanent structures, locations of fixtures, and customer traffic patterns. Each floor plan and store layout will vary according to the type of products sold, the building location, and how much the business can afford to put into the overall store design.

External Store Image

You don't always get a second chance to make a good first impression. The front of the store is usually consumers' first impression of the business—positive, negative, or neutral—influencing their decision to enter or not.

That said, sometimes consumers form that first impression long before they arrive at a store, through advertisements or word-of-mouth information. It is important, therefore, that all publicity and advertising projects the same image as the point of purchase. If a store's advertisements promote a sophisticated image, the store must have compatible positioning and visual effect.

Studies show that a store has fewer than seven seconds to capture the attention of passersby. A well-signed store with a nice window but too much merchandise visually polluting the entrance is not inviting to the consumer. In the same way, a clean and airy entrance does not guarantee traffic if the consumer cannot grasp the identity of the store.

Because retailers see their store every day, many end up losing their ability to see their stores with a critical eye. They allow merchandise to start piling up in windows and at the store entrance, projecting a confused image to the consumer. That scenario should always be avoided.

Exterior Design

A good external impression can compel a customer to enter a store. In general, it should be clear what a store sells from its entry, its storefront, its window, and any products that can be seen from outside. The store's vocation and target audience must be expressed outside the store.

That said, be careful not to be too bold with the store's architecture. Some stores that win "store of the year" award, end up closing in the following two years because their over-the-top exteriors scare customers away. You can be bold from your third store on—by then you will have earned a lot of experience.

The Storefront

Store design starts at the street to create a total experience for shoppers. The outside must reflect the inside. Anyone on the other side of the street should understand your business just by seeing your storefront. This seems banal and obvious, but many stores do not know to present themselves to pedestrians and especially to people speeding by in cars.

A retail store on a one-way street needs to take into account the direction of passing traffic and position the sign and the storefront slightly to that side.

A storefront needs to include, at the least, the name of the store, the type of trade (if it is not obvious), and a phone number. Any drawing that is not part of the logo is useless and will only make reading the sign difficult for anyone moving by quickly. Also, do not use the sign to tell the family story or explain the store's good qualities. Finally, choose a good name that cannot be confused with some other type of business. People will give your sign three seconds of their attention. If reading it requires more time than that, your sign will be useless.

The storefront has to be clean, clear, readable, and convincing. The sidewalk, too, must be clean and free from fixtures or ugly clutter. You'll never get customers into your store if the outside is uninviting.

The Entrance

When consumers decide to enter a store, most of them slow down to take a better look around. The first two steps inside a store form the area called the transition zone. This space should allow consumers to adapt to the store's lighting, temperature, and ambiance. At this point, they still don't completely know what products are displayed inside the store. So don't fill the door and the transition zone with merchandise; doing so only hinders consumers' entry and adaptation.

The entrance must be inviting, clear, and wide enough for a wheelchair or a mother with a stroller to enter. Customers hate standing anywhere that puts them at risk of other customers constantly brushing past them. In the transition zone, a little crowding can be useful, because it keeps people moving forward and into the store. However, in front of displays, crowding can be a big problem, because you want customers to linger in those areas. When they linger, they tend to buy more. So take a look at all the areas of customer flow in your store, from the entrance to the back of the store and out again, to see where you can make improvements.

This store inside a shopping mall has one door closed without reason. Never narrow the entrance of a store; you will be keeping consumers away needlessly.

The Window Display

The window display is an essential complement to store identification. With its window, a store makes a clear statement about what type of customers it wants to attract; trying to identify the store with many groups of customers will not please anyone.

All window displays should be dynamic and draw the eye. The entire window or its products should be changed every fifteen days, at least.

More than any area of a store except its displays of high-demand products, the window reflects the image and the marketing style of a store. Consumers can even guess the prices of certain stores by their style. In fact, the specific decoration doesn't matter if it reflects a consistent image to the general public. For example, if a pair of jeans is displayed beside a cotton shirt and a leather classic shoe it will reach an elegant public; if it is displayed with T-shirts and sneakers, it will reach a younger audience.

The window display needs to be well planned in advance to avoid any number of visibility problems after its assembly. The designer for the window display should consider the space's depth and length, which side of passing cars will be closest to the window, the flow of pedestrians, the distance between products and pedestrians, the reflectiveness of the glass, lighting effects, colors, themes, etc.

The display should incorporate innovative materials, backgrounds, and textures that do not overshadow the products and the products should be separated according to the interests of consumers. Some stores with large windows subdivide them, allowing a few feet of glass for each supplier; the result is a window divided with conflicting ideas and materials. It is better to have a single image plane, so that every supplier can project the same level of ambiance to the person who sees the display from the outside.

A seasonal window (coordinating with a special date or season) needs to be more daring than competitors' windows; always bringing to the theme "something more" that makes people stop and think. It should be connected to a similar campaign in the media, and the theme must be consistent between the two. The window should reflect the advertisement in its more exciting details, creating a visual connection between the advertising and the merchandising of the product.

Always be sure to check your stock of any products you display in the window. If you don't have a product you display, or if you have only a few sizes, you'll leave consumer profoundly frustrated. There is nothing worse than asking for an item displayed in the window and learning that it's no longer available, or to see a display for a special promotion that unfortunately "just finished."

Impellers

An impeller (high-sales) product should be displayed to attract the sale of other, less important products. Those other products will benefit from their privileged position due to sales of the successful product. The impellers are generally necessary consumption products or market leaders.

Some retailers place impellers near the front store door to attract flow. But if a retailer places cheap, common products at the door to attract the customers, that technique may attract the wrong customers and keep away the right ones.

When your business is located on a popular street, you can use some of that front space for products with a low profit margin. However, you really should not fill a prime position at the front of the store with cheap products; this detracts from the image of the store. Instead choose a higher-quality item that is equally attractive to the consumer. The best strategy is to use that space for new launches or for products that have been advertised in the media.

A basket is a promotional display that works well if you have just one product type with a brand and price indicator. If you mix different products in the same basket, you are making a mess, not a promotion.

Interior Design

The design of a store's interior space is important for three main reasons: it facilitates the purchase process; it balances the flow of traffic in accordance with customers' attraction to various categories; and it creates specific areas for promotional activity. In addition to the necessary visual elements, a store also must provide good means of access for all customers (e.g., ramps or automatic doors).

The environment inside the store is very important, and the store's design should take into consideration elements like gondolas and other fixtures, which should be chosen in accordance with the store's style and décor. The shelving should allow customers to see all that is offered, and all offerings—whether they're placed on the aisles, on the endcaps, or on islands—should be tagged with colored labels that can be read in the blink of an eye.

Inside the Store

The interior of a store is considered an internal window. The main items displayed in a store's window should also be arranged in a space inside, just after the transition zone. The window display invites consumers inside to meet a product personally, and this meeting must happen as quickly as possible so as not to block the customer's initial impulse.

Example 1: I see a lovely purple blouse in a store window, but when I enter the store and see nothing purple around, I realize that if I want to try on the blouse or check its quality, I will have to ask a clerk. Discouraged, I give up and leave the store.

Example 2: I see a lovely purple blouse in a store window. I enter the store, and just inside I see the purple blouses. I immediately go to them, feel the fabric, and then try one on. A salesperson notices my interest and closes the sale.

When you display an outfit in a window or on a mannequin, you should put the collection nearby so the consumer can easily touch the clothing and try it on. That is half the sale.

Sales Area

A store should be divided into specific areas depending on the sales they generate. Hot areas are the ones where sales are higher than the store average. Cold areas are the ones where sales are lower than the store average, like corners (dead spots), the area near the exit, and spaces that have little lighting or are outside the customer's visual field.

You can improve the profitability of cold areas by locating extra promotion spots there or directing traffic flow there through the use of gondolas, lighting, and signage. In short, use cold areas for sale items or products at their seasonal peak.

Identifying the Hot Areas

Before you decide where to put shelves and display fixtures, it is necessary to determine the most attractive places in the store. Just as there are rules for finding the most attractive location in a city, in a neighborhood, or on a block, there are rules for the best locations inside a store. These are the places where retailers should place their most important goods. In general, the best areas in a store are the most visible walls, intersections, the ends of aisles, areas of impact, and structural elements that can be used as focal points. Another place that deserves attention is the area around the checkout, which is ideal for impulse products.

Product Displays

It is useless to have a fantastic storefront, an inviting entrance, and a well-calculated layout if the merchandise is carelessly displayed. Displaying merchandise is more than just filling the shelves. Efficient merchandising requires constant discipline. The products must be separated by category (items exclusively for men, babies, winter, etc.).

In retail, good displaying follows several rules:

- Merchandise should be categorized in a way that makes it easy for consumers to guide themselves and choose products.
- The display equipment should be positioned to direct the traffic flow toward the center and back of the store, with the most attractive items at the ends of aisles. The design should allow for comfortable traffic flow and easy visibility for clerks, so they can follow what is happening and provide fast service.
- The merchandise should be organized. Just as it is necessary to organize a store's sections or departments, it is also necessary to organize its goods, whether by brand, price, size, or style.

(Bernardino, E. et al., Marketing de Varejo, *116)*

Circulation

A store's circulation should allow for the free flow of consumers among the gondolas and display racks. Any path should not have an end or barrier from which the consumer has to go back. When customers understand the sequence of the categories of displayed products, they feel at home and mentally record the layout during their visit. This intimacy with the store layout encourages them to return and make another purchase. When customers are lost and can't find the products they are looking for, they might ask for help, but doing so makes them feel unwelcome. A well-planned store makes shoppers' lives easier, and shoppers will return the favor by becoming loyal customers.

In general, the aisles must be easy to navigate, with free traffic flow between them. All aisles should be open at both ends; otherwise, customers will turn back before they reach the end. Consumers should be drawn toward the back of the store and feel that they are being guided by a path that leads to all categories. Consumers do not like to feel trapped or lost. They like to feel at home and like they can find what they need easily, even if it is their first visit to the store.

Learning to set up a store by leveraging the available spaces is simple, but pleasing frequent customers gets a little more complicated. It is important to understand that the layout should not be developed based on aesthetics alone. It must be functional to facilitate traffic flow and meet the wants and needs of consumers.

See how this wire dump bin interrupts the circulation? The resulting optical illusion is that there is not enough space to pass (even though there is), causing most consumers to turn back rather than continuing down the aisle.

A large display in the aisle creates a barrier that makes customers turn back, especially if they're just browsing. A store's passages and aisles should be clearly open, with no barriers in the customers' way. Any large barrier will seem like an impediment to their passage.

A product that is displayed in a high-traffic area will definitely sell more than its competitors in a lower-traffic location. When designing a layout, therefore, you must take into account not only the marketing of the products but also the value of each space. By doing so, you will achieve higher profitability per square meter.

There are small stores that are sales champions, while others with more space have lost their profitability by not knowing how to develop a good store layout.

Developing or Changing a Layout

When you develop a layout, you must try to please the majority of your customers, taking into account the type and class of consumers who you are seeking to target.

The layout should be planned on the basis of customers' gender, education, social class, and age, as well as the available space. The layout of a grocery store with upper-class patrons may not be the same as that with lower class patrons.

The layout has to be practical and should be periodically modified without major reforms. For small stores, especially, a periodic change in layout is important to ensure that the consumer senses constant improvement in the atmosphere of the store. In supermarkets, however, major changes need to be well calculated, because shoppers get used to the layout inside the store and do not like radical change.

Retailers should warn consumers before any such change, and they should use clear signs and a helpful, friendly staff to indicate the new positions of products or aisles.

How to Use Store Space

1. The store should be a continuation of the display window. Never allow barriers, such as closed doors, narrow doors, stairs, or any other obstacles to block customers' entry to the store.
2. Value all spaces; create elements of interest in each zone, with impactful displays in cold regions like the corners and back of the store.
3. The products must be better lit than the aisles.
4. Position the products to facilitate their handling; notice the angle of vision and handle points.
5. Support fixtures and other such equipment must be hidden. Consumers should see only merchandise.
6. Make customers comfortable with air conditioning, mirrors, seating, water, etc.
7. Installment credit counters should be at the back of the store, if possible, forcing the traffic flow in that direction.
8. Dressing rooms and gondolas with smaller products should be next to checkouts to prevent theft.

Merchandising Tips for Stores

*   Place high-turnover products away from the entrance and exits.
*   Don't put promotions at the entrance of a supermarket. They will disrupt access, and consumers who just entered the store won't be interested.
*   Essential consumer products should be positioned in places where the consumer is forced to pass through the largest possible number of aisles, but use good signage to indicate the products' location so customers won't get irritated and leave.
*   Make the checkout lanes wide enough for larger customers to pass through without embarrassment.
*   Promotions should be spaced out to avoid congestion and confusion. Promotions with taste samples should be placed far away from each other to avoid turmoil.

- Excessive bureaucracy during checkout affects a store's image. Cashiers must work quickly and avoid embarrassing customers at this delicate moment.
- Passing through the checkout as they leave the store is the last contact customers remember. Hire friendly, respectful cashiers, and do not complicate the payment process.
- Do not complicate the choice of products.
- Don't make your customers work. Discounted shoes should be attached in pairs, products with freebies must be easy to choose and take, etc.
- Never humiliate your customers, regardless of socioeconomic status. Give the customer making the smallest purchase the same comfort and attention you would give to someone buying an expensive product. Buying something, however small, feels great. Don't ruin the moment.
- Make the price tags and signage readable.
- Keep the bathrooms clean and fragrant; straighten the fitting rooms between customers.
- All merchandise should be orderly.

Do not sell a mess. Place sales merchandise in order, or grouped in a promotional basket for the same price.

Store Operation

Retailers have the daily challenge of offering their customers a mix of products: popular and desirable, or efficient and cost-effective. Merchandising should be used as a tool to generate high traffic and high profits, thus increasing a store's competitive advantage, boosting sales, and clearing out the stock of any product.

Logistics

Many retailers are looking for ways to increase their profitability. Improved financial results often depend on cost reduction and the rationalization and optimization of processes. All the operations related to the management of merchandise and materials — the planning and control of production, packaging, storage, physical distribution, shipping, transportation, and communication systems—are called logistics.

Activities related to logistics:
- customer service
- sales forecasting
- location of factories and warehouses
- communication/information
- supplies
- production planning
- production order
- inventory control
- material handling
- storage
- packaging
- transportation
- handling of discarded products
- disposition of scrap

The logistics of retail have advanced, resulting in reduced costs; less waste; optimization of the purchasing, production, and distribution of merchandise; and optimization of each step in the marketing chain. With the computerized registration of documents and merchandise, retailers have seen a number of benefits, including automatic management of inventories, reduced paperwork, and the elimination of typographical errors.

In addition to new logistics tools, there are new technological resources that support all operations of receipt, storage, and delivery. Among them are management software that automatically indicate where merchandise should be stored or removed; routing systems that help decrease travel time for delivery vehicles; satellite trackers that monitor the paths of trucks; and on-board computers that direct communication between drivers and the company.

CHAPTER 4:
THE GONDOLA

Gondolas

Gondolas are the stands that sustain the shelves used in self-service systems. Their dimensions should be proportional to the size of the area and the height of the store ceiling. Very long shelves (more than eight meters) tire consumers, and very short ones distract them.

The height of the shelves must be proportional to the style of the store and the quantity of merchandise that you want to expose. Any merchandise on a shelf higher than 2 m (6 ft. 5 in.) from the floor will be out of reach of consumers; therefore very high shelves should be reserved for stock. In wholesale stores, it's very common to use shelves up to 4 m high, but a supermarket that wants its products to be visually pleasing to consumers should not go above 2 m. Retailers should take into consideration not only the product category but the average height of the customers who will attempt to reach the product in question. The store that has gondolas up to 1.8 m (6 ft.) high seems more expansive and pleasant than a similar store with taller fixtures.

Items that generate higher profits should be positioned in the middle of the gondola, in the area where consumers stop scanning the line of products when they walk into the aisle. That way the client will examine the products in order, from the cheapest to the most expensive or vice-versa. The store will choose which way is more effective for their customers.

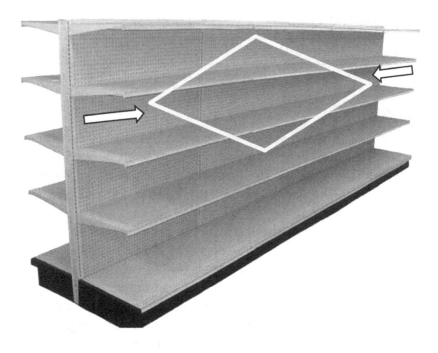

The gondola and its best places.

The most visible area of a gondola or an aisle is the middle.

Shelves

Shelves should be chosen according to the product line. They should provide space for larger and smaller packages, in a variety of quantities. They must be made of durable material (no glass) and always with a movable rack system that allows you to adjust height. Fixed shelves sacrifice products that do not fit, and they leave lots of holes without any product. This means lost space and, consequently, lost profitability.

Why avoid glass? After all, glass is a very beautiful material that gives a clean view of the store. Stores that are sophisticated or that carry little merchandise can use glass. But fast retail and stores full of products, such as supermarkets and drugstores, shouldn't. Employees tend to avoid moving glass shelves for fear of breaking them (even when there is a rack to adjust the height). As a result, the store maintains the same shelf capacity and looks the same forever.

Gondola Arrangement

Global food retail is light-years ahead of other retail in terms of merchandising experience; this industry and its actions offer a wealth of information about effective display strategies that maximize sales productivity per square foot.

Every product in every kind of store should be displayed regardless of its size, and the shelves should always be filled to the top, leaving space for fingers so the consumer can reach in and pick up the product. Don't display a package that is 10 cm tall on a shelf that is 40 cm high, leaving 30 cm of empty space; that's a loss of space and displayed products. This kind of arrangement is only acceptable if the shelves are fixed and the person who arranges the products does not know any way to improve the display. If the products are too short for the shelf space, buy more shelves and try to optimize the space with more products per square centimeter.

To get a satisfactory shelf presentation, place every product facing forward. Do not allow the product to be displayed on its side, upside down, backward, or in any other position that impairs the consumer's ability to see the product or read the label.

To obtain a good arrangement, determine the number of product fronts (or faces) that will fit on the shelf according to the size of the packaging. Never display a single package (one front) if the product is small. The more packages, the better the display, because consumers will have a better impression of the product.

Following the direction of greater traffic flow on a particular aisle, always display big products after the small ones. This arrangement allows for better visualization, because the bigger products won't hide the smaller ones. Group together all the sizes of the same product, and always strive for order and alignment by packaging. This helps consumers identify a particular line or product more quickly.

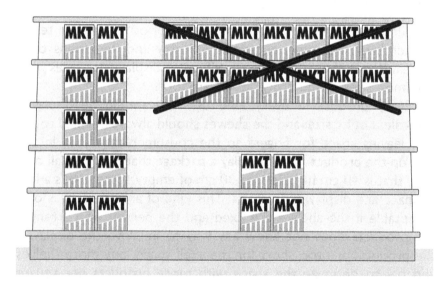

We can make three types of arrangement: vertical, horizontal and blocky.

Vertical

The best and most beautiful arrangement is vertical, when the same product occupies all the shelves from bottom to top, with equal fronts. This type of display has a greater visual impact, provides clarity for customers who choose the product, and facilitates picking up the product.

There is a simple explanation for why we take in vertical displays more quickly and easily than we do horizontal ones. Our eyes focus on a central point more easily when the image in question is narrow. When the image is long and horizontal, our eyes have to move from left to right, as if we're reading, and so it takes time to understand the whole image. As a result, a product displayed vertically is perceived much more quickly than if it were displayed horizontally.

The best arrangement is vertical, with four or more products on each shelf. It is not possible to do a vertical arrangement with only one package per shelf. This creates a "strip" that consumers won't notice.

A vertical arrangement is the best type for visual perception.

Horizontal

A horizontal arrangement—with a long line of the same product on one shelf—is not recommended because it confuses the eye. It takes customers longer to perceive a product in this formation when they're scanning the shelves.

Nevertheless, horizontal arrangements are frequently used for products displayed on a single shelf. After people learned about the benefit of displaying products at eye level, some suppliers wanted to use horizontal arrangements to take advantage of that fact. But when a product arrangement starts horizontally, all the other products around it have to be arranged the same way. The resulting lines of products disturb shoppers' vision and make it difficult for them to search the various brands or flavors.

In the food market, some stores make a planogram displaying premium brands or products with high profit margin potential on the highest shelf, while value-priced items are generally presented on lower shelves. It's strange ... who decided that rich people are tall and poor people are short?

Horizontal might be the quickest way to arrange products, but it's the worst to consumers' eyes.

Blocky

The alternative option to the previous ones is the block arrangement. If space is limited and there is no way to put the product vertically, the best option is to arrange the products in blocks. This arrangement is average in terms of merchandising effectiveness, but sometimes it's the only option when there's a lack of shelf space. In a block arrangement, products are placed side by side, forming small blocks of two or more shelves, which at least allows for good visibility. Currently, with the use of new software for space management and the lack of shelf spaces for many products, this type of arrangement prevails.

A block arrangement, while not ideal, is better than a horizontal arrangement. Break colors to help highlight each block of product.

When you are preparing a shelf display, remember these rules:

- Turn all the packages with their best sides to the front. Check to make sure that the products' names and brands are visible.
- Make sure the price tags are positioned below the correct products.
- Group subcategories (or for example flavors) in order.
- Following the direction of the greater traffic flow, put the smaller packages at the beginning of the shelves and the larger ones at the ends.
- Place small packages on the top shelves and the bigger, heavier ones on the bottom shelves.
- *Never* display products of the same category in separate places.
- *Never* store low-turnover products to occupied empty shelves.

Wrong arrangement. Packages that are not oriented to the consumer are usually ignored in self-service. It's far better to put products facing forward than sideways. If you plan well, the gondola will have space for almost the same number of products with their main side to the front.

Self-Service Product Positioning

Every product planogram in a store should have the same four goals: separation, visibility, accessibility, and availability.

All items must be separated by categories according to gondola location, or how the consumer looks for it. We can then separate the products by type, gender, size, color, price, style, etc. The more difficult it is for customers to find products on the shelves, the more staff will be needed to help these "lost" customers.

Products should not only be separated by category; they should also be visible from at least three meters away. If a product is small, display it in large quantities so that it is noticeable. Products that are badly displayed or are hard to see don't sell. When a product shows a lower turnover than normal, change places to see if that fixes the problem. Poor access is synonymous with low visibility.

A good display brings a lot of advantages: it makes shopping easier, saves time, reminds people of needed items, and breaks the visual monotony.

Products planograms are projected to maximize the gondola space and explore buying trends.

Endcaps

Endcaps are traditionally promotional spots.

When retailers make an endcap the extension of a shelf or put secondary items on it, they are wasting the attention of the consumer, who is used to endcap promotions, and wasting valuable space that could be used for more profitable products. Ideally, an endcap will have only one type of product or one line of products, with big visible information and prices. If it is not possible to devote that much space to a single product or line, retailers can put up to three related products there but no more. Many stores put several products on each endcap, which confuses the customer and kills the eye-catching effect.

On the left, an empty, wasted endcap; on the right, a confusing, improperly arranged endcap. Both are a waste of money.

The strongest display points are endcaps, where customers are forced to walk around the end of the gondola, almost stopping in front of the endcap for a moment. When they are turning they see all sides of the endcaps, so never left holes on the sides.

An endcap has three sides, and all three sides must be filled. Both endcaps here are displaying the same number of products. Does it look that way?

This is a perfect endcap project, with an effective use of communication and products. (From Tradezed.com.br).

Counters

Counters are ideal for controlled products or products that need refrigeration or heating. With the exception of drugstores, bakeries, and jewelry stores, however, most stores use the self-service system. Any product that does not need controlling should be displayed within reach of the customer.

Some stores fear being shoplifted and keep their products behind glass or even padlocked, but that is the fastest way to stop selling. A product behind glass has less chance of being bought than a product with easy access. It may seem silly, but having to ask for a product is a barrier to impulse buying.

Which do you prefer—selling two beers a day and not having any stolen or selling forty-nine beers a day but losing one to a shoplifter?

Stacking

If retailers plan to stack products on the floor, they must observe the following rules:

- The pile should be isolated from the ground by a base or a pallet.
- The pile must be well assembled and balanced to prevent collapse.
- An oversized pile or perfect organization discourages buyers, who will fear disassembling the display.
- The product should always be within reach of any consumer, even if the pile is large.
- Do not leave the merchandise at the top of a pile too organized, because again, an impeccable arrangement intimidates the customer.

Stacked displays should always be set on a pallet, the products should be easy to pick up, and the display should include a promotional sign indicating the price.

Pallets

Pallets are platforms on which merchandise is stacked. Specially built for transport by forklift, they are used for high-turnover or promotional products, or to give the appearance of large numbers. Supermarkets use them to demarcate an island and facilitate night refitting with a forklift.

Pallets must be covered with pallet wrap or strips of shelf paper, especially if they are in bad condition. They should be positioned strategically so as not to hinder the normal flow of traffic in the area; essentially they create a new extra spot for products.

Cleaning

All products, without exception, must give the impression of quality to the consumer. The place where the products and fixtures (gondolas, etc.) are displayed must also look absolutely clean.

Ensuring cleanliness of the products and display shelves during the supply process is very important. There are still stores that leave dented, dusty, or ripped packages on the shelves because they will not accept the loss.

But the image of the store and its products are destroyed by such carelessness. Customer rejection is something that can be seen in the details. In groceries, medicine, health and beauty products, and most other retail segments, packaging cannot be sticky or dusty because it will disgust consumers, who generally reject any product in this condition. In a purchasing environment, all displays and printed materials must be absolutely clean, as well.

Managing Spaces

Putting the right product (for the consumer) in the right position and in the right quantity is the basic goal of space management, which has been increasing in strategic importance for many retail chains and suppliers. For this reason, stores should carefully control space in this valuable and busy piece of "promotional real estate"—the point of purchase.

Thousands of new products are launched every year, yet the shelf space for displaying them remains the same. As a result, intracategory disputes occur when products of the same category compete for space within the category itself, and intercategory disputes occur when new product categories are launched. Retailers must award space to the products that really deserve it.

For supermarket owners, gut instinct and experience administering store spaces (gondolas, shelves, and extra spots) may not be sufficient to ensure the best return on an investment in space. High customer interest, narrow profit margins, fierce competition, and more demanding consumers require professional guidance and some technological assistance (such as modern planograms software) to manage store spaces in the most profitable manner.

Currently, you can't talk about space management without also considering the use of software programs that help with product organization and calculate the exact return on each item displayed on the gondola. With this kind of software, stores stop losing sales, because their shelves are always stocked according to consumer convenience. The planograms (layout of gondolas) generated by these systems highlight the profitability of each product, which is one of the fundamental factors determining competitive advantage in retail.

The increasing use of computerized methods to assess the performance of shelves should put an end to the practice of retailers and suppliers negotiating over commercial space.

Although this software gives an accurate assessment of whether it's justifiable to display a certain product on the shelf, the store manager should use common sense to determine whether or not consumers will miss the product if it's not displayed. Even with all the technology available to them, the destination of a particular product is still literally in the hands of retail managers.

Planograms are generated from pictures of products and an analysis of their display situation depending on the sales of each type of product. They project the best position for each product and the number of days of inventory to keep on hand to avoid rupture.

The planogram software helps retailers maximize profitability through product mixing, redefining and repositioning gondola arrangements.

Planogram

A planogram is a diagram or drawing that provides detailed information about where every product in a retail store should be placed. These schematics not only present a flow chart for the particular merchandise departments within a store layout, but also show on which aisle and on what shelf a particular item should be located. A planogram should also illustrate how many facings are allocated for each SKU (stock keeping unit).

The complexity of a planogram may vary according to the size of the store, the software used to create it, and the need of the retailer.

This planogram software is offered by Planogrambuilder.com.

Creation of Planograms

Big-box stores and larger retailers typically hire merchandising specialists to assist in developing planograms, or they may have their own in-house planogrammers. Because of the hefty price of most planogram software, small and independent retailers often resort to using word processors or paper and pen to optimize shelf layout.

Small stores don't need planogram software or a technical staff to manage space. An effective planogram can be as simple as a photo of each preset section (side of the gondola) to give the retailer a sense of each space and the categories placed there. With a computer, retailers can include details about each product, including facing numbers and the exact placement of each item.

As competition among products increases, vendors and distributors are becoming more aware of the importance of correctly merchandising their products. That awareness is leading to better point of sale displays, planograms and other marketing aids provided to retailers directly by the suppliers at no cost.

Planogram Purpose

Product placement and improved sales are just two very basic reasons retailers should be implementing planograms in their shops. Planograms provide many other positive benefits, including these:

- more visual appeal to customers
- tighter inventory control and reduction of out-of-stock items
- easier product replenishment for staff
- more logical product positioning
- more effective communication regarding staff-produced displays
- facilitation of consumers' choices
- optimal utilization of each centimeter of shelf space based on sales volume and profit margins

Any good retailer realizes that the key to increased sales is proper merchandising. A planogram is one of the best merchandising tools for presenting products to the customer. If you aren't using planograms, it may be time to start.

Small Stores

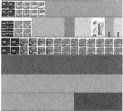

Medium Stores

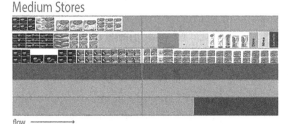

Supermarkets

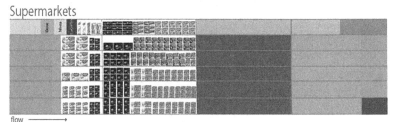

This is a three-size planogram, to serve different stores and different product assortments.

Making and Keeping a Planogram

It's well known that there is a strong correlation between a shelf display—the number of fronts exposed and the product's position in the gondola—and the consequent rotation of that product. Therefore many suppliers are giving full support to stores to ensure and increase their share in the market. Product category planograms comes to help.

Making a planogram can be compared to playing a chess game or solving a math problem. The intention is to achieve the best result with the fewest movements possible.

3-D planograms. The correct ones present your products and your competitor's.

In Europe, supermarkets generally work with eighty to one hundred different categories. They make two annual revisions, which translates to a thousand different planograms per year. A single planogram analyst might take care of one hundred fifty to two hundred. For this reason, it is very difficult to coordinate all the variables in their work, which focuses on movements of new products (inputs) as well as modifications (outputs or exchanges).

Some industries conduct deep research into consumer behavior in each type of store. Then they collaborate with retail chains and other strategically interesting stores, suggesting research-based planograms to help eliminate the doubts in retail.

In practice, few brands can find retailers willing to go with a complete (top-to-bottom) vertical display by brand. As shelf space is scarce in all stores, planograms usually provide for vertical blocks of products. An extensive product line can have a main block dedicated to that brand, separated by flavors, colors, or types.

The correct arrange of products is by sales performance (i.e., put products that sell more at or near eye level, and those that sell less on the lower shelves).

The arrangement of products on the shelves—that is, their visibility—is a crucial aspect of sales optimization. The correct location must answer the following criteria:

- Products placed above head level constitute 9 percent of sales. Many are outside customers' reach and visual range.

- Products placed at eye level represent more than 52 percent of sales, so more profitable products—those from which a retailer wants greater output—should be placed in this area.
- Products placed at hands height (where it is easy to handle them) occupy the second place in total sales, at 26 percent.
- Products located near the floor (bottom shelf) represent less than 13 percent of sales.

The "visual comfort zone" at gondolas height, which is the one that we best visualize, without us having to move our eyes or heads, is between our head and hands. A research conducted by Nielsen in 2007 (Strunck, "Antropometria, ergonomia e planogramas") has shown that the products at eyes and hands level have higher sales comparing to products that lie above or below this area, transforming this space, into the most disputed in the shelves, especially in auto service.

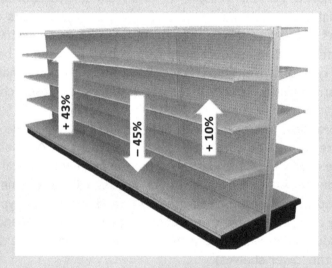

Products on the bottom shelf, when placed in a higher position, have their sales increased by 43 percent. Those on the penultimate shelf, when placed one shelf higher, have 10 percent increased sales. On the other hand, products that have been relegated to the bottom shelf lose 45 percent! This only proves that we buy what we see... and our eyes are lazy.

A research report from RIS News examines how many retailers have a problem with in-store merchandising accuracy. Anecdotal evidence from discussions with merchandisers indicate the problem is large and is supported by the research report that found only 3.7 percent of retailers have exact accuracy of planogram knowledge down to the fixture level for all their stores.

Retailers have lost confidence in their stores' ability to execute localized campaigns quickly and effectively. In addition, communication from headquarters to stores typically lacks timeliness and relevance.

With the right suite of visual merchandising management solutions, an accurate merchandising planning process is attainable. With these tools, communication becomes clear and precise, and retailers save time and money. Visual merchandising management solutions enable retailers access to real-time information needed to carry out accurate localized campaigns to their stores.

When the right product and messaging is delivered to the right store, at the right time, on the right fixture, retailers can drive the customer experience envisioned in the original planning process.

A quarter of retailers say they do not measure store execution and compliance regularly. Seven percent only measure it once or twice a year and a much larger group (18.5 percent) say they never do it at all. However, three in ten retailers report measuring store-level compliance frequently enough to catch problems and correct them.

Aside from budget constraints, which are always a high-wire act of balancing competing priorities, the biggest inhibitor to solving non-compliance problems is a "disconnect between merchandising, marketing and store operations," according to nearly 54 percent of respondents.

Sadly, the king of in-store merchandise planning, communication and compliance tools today is Excel. By a landslide majority, Excel (63 percent) was named the solution most retailers use for in-store merchandise planning. However, one of the major takeaways is that use of Excel in merchandising operations is a known problem in compliance efforts at the fixture level. The silver lining is that these problems are solvable once a comprehensive solution is adopted, and will result in significant sales and margin benefits once compliance is met.

Today, the bulk of the retailing industry is operating with known data gaps, inaccuracies at the store level and workaround tools that are sorely in need of upgrading. Merchandising plans and forecasts are based on historical or aggregated averages that are essentially guesswork instead of hard science. The ultimate solution is to tie customer-centric improvements in the store with in-store merchandising improvements that increase sales, conversions and customer satisfaction while enabling efforts to reduce waste and lost opportunities.

(www.risnews.edgl.com)

How Categories Boost Sales

Category management and divisions in a sector are ways to define product assortment, prices, offers, and promotions to serve different consumers and maintain consistency in the way that products are presented in retail according to consumers' affinity. This facilitates customer purchases and generates an increase in sales. The universe of product categories can be divided into four concepts that ensure good profitability by expanding the category management philosophy and leading to consistently higher sales. They are destination, routine, convenience, and seasonality.

Destination categories signal to the consumer the competitive position of the store. They are directly related to the store's comparatively greater variety of products and lower prices, and to the space and comfort that the customer will find in the store.

Routine categories include items purchased regularly. If well exploited, these sales generate a competitive edge as well as cash. They create a positive image of the store brand and help build customer loyalty, because customers know that they will find what they need at that location. In the routine categories, prices do not need to be the lowest, but they should be competitive.

Convenience categories include products that consumers don't normally buy at that store—for example, products consumers don't need but will buy on impulse when they see them at the checkout or when they're searching for something else. If well exploited by the retailer, these categories refer consumers to what the experts call *store of choice*, creating the feeling that they will find what they need there.

Finally, **seasonal** categories include products used during a particular season of the year. These categories of products also can give consumers the impression that they can find everything they need in a certain store, making the store a point of reference.

To manage these categories properly, it is necessary to identify the needs of a store's consumers and to determine which categories would be best for the store and whether the categories need more investment or expansion.

How Categories Changes by Retail Type

The same product that is placed in one category in one retail business can be placed in another category in another type of store. For example, a cereal bar would be in the destination category in a supermarket, but it would be in the convenience category in a drugstore.

Retail Is Detail

Here we have two examples of cheese shelf arrangements. Which one do you prefer? Which one do you think has higher-quality products?

There are several important facts about the value of space in various sectors of a store:
- Avoid monotony by mixing the colors of similar packages and organizing boxes by size.
- Observe the entire display area to analyze the final effect. Look at the whole area from a distance of four meters. When placing products, retailers should have a real concept of what the consumer sees when entering the aisle, so they should check the display from a distance.

- As most people are right-handed, the products that lend themselves to impulse purchasing should be positioned to the right of the main product (the leader) for easier access.

Of course the stores in these photos are different, but that is not the problem here. Which store has arranged its product to inspire impulse purchases and appeal to the appetite? A good display is not necessarily a question of paying more money, but the general appearance of a display can affect whether customers trust the quality of the products.

What does a well-displayed product mean for you?

Do I need to ask this man if he sells watermelons? No, it's obvious that he does. But when I can't reach the product or see the price, will I make a quick decision to buy?

Look closely at the picture on this page. The watermelons here are being "super displayed," but they cannot be picked up, their price isn't clearly marked, and the salesperson is showing no interest in helping customers (he's filing his nails). In short, it is not enough for a product to have good exposure; it must be well displayed, clearly priced, and easy to access, either via self-service or a helpful salesperson.

Regardless of the product, it must be displayed in sufficient quantity to be seen from four meters away, be immaculate in appearance and storage, be separated by type, have a legible price tag in the right place, and be easy to pick up and carry.

> **"Quality is not what the product claims to have, it is what the consumer recognizes and is willing to pay to have it."**
> **Peter Drucker**

CHAPTER 5:
PROMOTIONAL MARKETING

Promotional Actions

The desire to be closer to the consumer during the crucial moment of the purchase has attracted more companies to POP. However, before drawing up a plan of action, company leaders should have a clear understanding of their marketing strategy: what product they are marketing, what type of consumer that product should reach, and what are the best ways to distribute it.

Depending on their marketing strategy, executives have to answer the following questions:

- What must happen at the POP to serve the needs of the consumer?
- Who performs those functions (manufacturers, retailers, promotion or advertising agencies)?
- Who can perform those functions in the most effective manner in terms of cost and results?
- How should the product pricing structure reflect this allocation of functions?

Once these questions are answered, the marketing team can develop the plans, goals, agencies and media program budget.

What makes industries and stores take aggressive actions, are the well-known advantages of merchandising:

- increased sales and faster turnover
- measurable results
- an immediate return on investment
- consumer loyalty to the brand and the store
- potential division of costs between supplier and retailer

Promotional Environment

The promotional actions in the POP should be treated like a show, giving the audience/consumers a sense of happiness, relationship, novelty, and experimentation. Promotions at the POP should allow customers to experience a complete sensory tour, integrating sight, smell, hearing, taste, and touch. It is up to the merchandisers and marketers to entertain the customers and, in so doing, differentiate themselves from other brands. If the fun is properly directed, this stimulation will reap fantastic results in terms of sales and brand loyalty.

Planning and Implementation

The details of a promotion must be clearly defined: product, duration, space required, price, projected demand, merchandising materials, etc. For both retail and industry, it is necessary to create mechanisms and rational criteria by which to approve or reject a promotion.

The majority of promotions are hurried, disregarding the minimum time necessary to select personnel, conduct training, print promotional material, delivery to all stores, etc. These projects spend more time on the desks of executives than in the hands of the performers, who then must try to do the best possible job in record time.

Demand

Demand refers to how much (what quantity) of a product or service is desired by buyers at a certain price. The relationship between those variables—price and quantity—is known as the demand.

In economics, demand for a good or service is calculated as the total amount of a good or service that a market would choose to buy at every possible market price.

Merchandising ensures that stores stock enough of a product to meet demand without overstocking. To achieve that balance, merchandisers analyze a product's past sales performance and forecast future demand. They take into account advertising and marketing campaigns and seasonal factors that could influence short-term demand. By developing accurate forecasts, merchandisers ensure that stores can take advantage of sales opportunities while controlling costs and maintaining profit levels.

Conducting Promotions

Before we conduct a promotion, we should define what we plan to do, how we plan to do it, and how much it will cost. That information is needed in order to measure the results afterward. It is very common for retailers to launch a promotion even when it is not profitable, simply as a response to some promotion by a competitor. They feel undermined by the competitor, believing that the competitor is thriving as a result of the promotion, and they end up imitating it.

It is important for a retailer to know how to do calculations and forecasts before deploying any new promotion, because simply mimicking a competitor's promotion does not guarantee that it is the correct action or one will bring profitable results to that particular store. In order to be good in marketing, it is not enough to have intuition and creativity; it is necessary to perform measurements and calculations, without which a promotional action is just based on gut feelings.

Types of Promotional Actions for Suppliers and Retailers

Suppliers Helping Train Retail

When an industry distributes its products through different points of purchase that do not use the self-service system, its sales, image, and approach to the consumer depend heavily upon the store's attendants. By providing direct training to the retailer, a supplier guarantees that the employees who interact with consumers will know how to sell its product. Making the salesclerks excited about the supplier's brand and its quality brings short-term benefits and in the long term decreases the risk of a competitor overshadowing the supplier's products at that POP.

Supplier-provided training can be made available in a number of ways. For example, the supplier could develop a training program for all clerks involved with its products, or it could host a convention specifically to train retail employees in the operation of the product and/or specific sales techniques. A second way is to send trained promoters to each relevant POP to provide up to two hours of training to all employees who work in the store. The cheapest but least efficient method is to send training brochures and broadsheets to all the stores, hoping the employees read them.

The ideal strategy would be to host a convention for the large retailers, provide staff training for the medium retailers, and send flyers to the more distant or very small retailers. For innovative products or major launches, this type of multifaceted action is crucial.

And for retailers, such action on the part of suppliers is a good deal, because the industry investment in training comes at almost no cost to stores.

Relationship

A relationship action aims for a quick approach to the consumer. It wants to improve communications with its audience, be it another company (B to B, or business to business) or the final consumer (B to C, or business to consumer).

The main objectives are to break down barriers and to create a shared sense of empathy between both sides. It requires much perspicacity and psychology to achieve the right points of interest. A relationship action sometimes begins with a plentiful distribution of giveaways; and good will can improve the relationship and result in sales.

Education and Interaction for Consumption

For a long time, the cosmetic industries have promoted demonstrations of their products, teaching consumers how to experience their fragrances or choose a lipstick or put on makeup. These actions boost sales greatly, because they help the consumer understand and buy the product.

A promotional action in a retail environment allows for greater involvement of the consumer with the merchandise. A demonstration that teaches customers how a product works is a passive activity. For customers, it is much more interesting to play an active role—that is, to handle the product and find out how it works, which makes them feel more in command of the product. After interacting with the product, consumers become more confident in their decision to purchase it, as they already feel like they own it.

Loyalty Actions

Very similar to the relationship action, the loyalty action is a way for a company to get closer to shoppers or consumers. The difference is that it uses "rewards" to attract them. With loyalty actions, the consumer is given a sense of exclusivity through frequent-flyer or points programs with the promise of benefits or prizes.

Motivating Actions

Motivating actions reward the person who corresponds to certain standards established by the companies, in some type of promotional tool. Among the most famous motivating action is the "mystery shopper." Some companies undertake this type of action periodically to measure the performance of retail clerks or even their own employees. They often inform storeowners and their employees ahead of time that the mystery shopper will be visiting them; clerks who promote the company's product spontaneously can earn prizes.

Companies generally hire a merchandising or promotion agency to oversee the operation of a motivating action. Besides boosting the sales, these actions provide valuable feedback about what retailers know about the product, the level of their service, and how to improve the relationship between the supplier and the retailer.

Couponing

Couponing is the action of distributing coupons that consumers can redeem for discounts or special offers by the supplier or retailer (depending on who's paying for the coupons). The coupons can be distributed through newspapers, magazines, direct mail, store flyers, or the product package. This type of action is useful only if the coupons are directed to new consumers. If the coupons are used by the consumers who are already loyal to the product, the supplier or retailer will just be losing money.

Incentive

Incentive campaigns (which are part of relationship marketing) are those that set target sales goals and announce awards for performance, with the aim of improving results through motivation. Incentive campaigns may be directed toward retailers, wholesalers, distributors, or the companies' employees (sellers and promoters).

With this type of action, everybody who is involved in the campaign in any capacity should get the chance to win prizes.

When the company and retailer collaborate on an incentive program, the motivational forces are multiplied. With both sides interested in achieving their goals, sales get double the attention. Incentive campaigns usually reward participants with concert tickets, merchandise, trips, cars, or any other prize generally considered worth the extra effort. This type of campaign needs to be well planned to avoid any discredit or unrealistic expectations. The incentive should be applicable during a specified period (short- or long-term) or certain occasions. We should not amend a program to another program, in order not to scathe the company's image and not to create addiction in the participants.

Institutional

Institutional actions do not aim to sell. Instead they aim to reinforce or modify the image of a company or store, adding value to the institution and enhancing the corporate or brand image. Often the institution will sponsor a concert, exposition, festival, parade, marathon, sports competition, etc. To support the institutional advertising campaign, the company will offer giveaways or host cocktail parties or similar events. There are unlimited ways to publicly present a brand or a company in the best possible light without directly mentioning its products.

Cultural

Institutions will sometimes host exclusive events that take place on demand, or sponsor cultural events to provide the population or any specific group with access to concerts, exhibits, ballets, etc. For example, a performance by a metropolitan choir might be sponsored by Cepacol lozenges. Many of these events take place inside stores and shopping malls.

Demonstration

Demonstrations allow consumers to get to know and evaluate a product. This kind of personal contact in the POP is very effective; it's one of the in-store promotional actions that costumers tend to remember best. A well-trained demonstrator can increase product sales and ensure that about 40 percent of customers remember the product. Demonstrators should be well trained and should use simple, not technical language. The demonstration should also be strategically timed to reach the target audience. These types of actions do not need to be connected to a general program and can differ by store. Actions, such as demonstrations or tastings require advance preparation and coordinated scheduling with the stores in question.

Tasting

A tasting allows consumers to sample a certain food or drink. Usually demonstrators use special counters or trays to serve samples of the promoted product to interested consumers. The index of perception of this type of promotion can reach a striking 49 percent and can result in a very high increase in sales, depending on the type of product and the quality of the action. Tastings are ideal for product launches or the introduction of new flavors. Research by A. C. Nielsen showed that 83 percent of consumers would buy a product after a satisfactory tasting, regardless of price.

During a tasting, it is important to listen to and write down all consumer comments about the product to detect their level of satisfaction and approval. Often, this is equivalent to field research.

Observe coffee tastings in supermarkets. Some demonstrators speak about the brand and its quality and distribute brochures so that consumers will remember what they drank. The majority, unfortunately, simply distribute the coffee to anyone who approaches. Without giving any information about the tasted product, the action is just a waste of money.

Sampling

Sampling is the distribution of free product samples in small packages just like the original, or in small portions. The object of a sampling is to introduce a newly launched product or to enlarge the number of people who are familiar with the product, reinforcing its image and increasing its consumers. Putting a product into the hands of consumers helps them know and identify it without having to purchase it first. This accelerates sales results and extends the consumer market for the product. Samplings can be held in stores, door to door, at universities, in hospitals, at sporting events or fairs, etc. All distributed samples must be accompanied by a small, explanatory brochure to facilitate understanding by the consumer, who does not always want to hear a message directly from the promoter.

It is very common to see bakeries distributing cakes and bread samples to promote new flavors. This may sound like an extra expense to some people, but it is truly an investment in future sales.

Cross Sampling

Cross sampling is a technique that uses a product with great market penetration to publicize another unknown product. The unknown product is "taking a ride" with the known one so buyers have an opportunity to try the new product. The hitchhiker product always assimilates some of the qualities of reliability already earned by the successful product.

Giveaways or Promotional Bundles

A giveaway can generate a large sales flow for a product, but many companies make the mistake of failing to properly show or explain how consumers can win the giveaway. Below we have an example of this kind of mistake: the bag is well displayed, but customers don't know what they must buy in order to win it. Sometimes only a single promoter in the POP can answer questions about a promotion. Retailers cannot assume that consumers know about the company's promotional plans. In-store promotions should be explained simply and meticulously, and the store should train all employees in preparation for every campaign that happens in the POP.

A lone giveaway product at the gondola, without explanation or promotional material, means nothing to the consumer.

Store Flyer Promotions

Flyers are an excellent vehicle for advertising and promotion. Many consumers say that they choose a store by its flyers and promotions. A flyer with valuable promotions builds customer loyalty, while the flyer with misleading promotions loses the attention and loyalty of customers over time.

Actions in the Packaging

Manufacturers frequently use promotions to make buying a more exciting activity. They might include giveaways, coupons, free samples, or other product offers in their packaging to make their products stand out among the competition. But some stores don't understand the idea, and they display those promotions in the worst places in the gondolas, killing the effect. Retailers must understand that these packages are intended to make customers happy with the brand and with the store, too.

Cooperative Advertising

Retailers can choose to advertise any of their products in the media. Sometimes they can split the cost of advertising with suppliers by means of a cooperation agreement. With cooperative advertising, the supplier pays for all or part of the promotion. In general, based on a percentage of the invoice, suppliers may grant subsidies in cash or products to participate in media advertisements or store flyers.

Contests and Sweepstakes

Contests are promotional actions in which consumers compete for a prize or a voucher giveaway by answering a question on paper and either depositing the paper in a ballot box or sending it in by mail or via internet.

Some actions require a complicated routine—you have to buy a certain product first and get the receipt stamped by the cashier, or you have to turn a roulette wheel, or you must answer a long questionnaire—and they do not get good results, because the complicated process turns away consumers. Keep it simple!

Looking for Customers Outside the Store

There are many reasons why the flow of people in a store might suddenly decrease. If the reasons are not seasonal or known, the retailer must first look for the reasons in the store's billing. If the reason still isn't clear, the retail staff needs to organize to attract another type of customer. One solution is to create a team that goes to companies, factories, clubs, organizations, churches, etc., to seek potential customers. To do this, the team needs to have a package of promotional materials that explains why people should patronize the store and take advantage of its good service. The team can begin with some flyers, a good telemarketing service, suppliers' catalogues, fast home delivery, discounts for people on the select company's payroll, or temporary booths in factories to win the trust of the employees.

It is common for a supplier to participate in events and, such as city fairs, concerts in parks, rodeos, etc., to take advantage of the public gathering with promotional acts, distribution of brochures or samples, demonstrations, or tastings. Usually, some supplier will set up a booth at the event with some special attraction or program inviting free public participation. The retailer should participate, too, to strengthen its brand and public image outside the store.

Selling Spaces for Actions in POP

A supplier's promotional budget includes the fees it pays to use the space inside a retail store. Currently, the sale of space in stores is not considered illegal; however, it is considered unethical in certain circumstances. The rates suppliers pay vary depending on the nature of the product, the interest of the manufacturer, and the relative power of the retailer. In theory, the brands that command high consumer loyalty should pay lower rates, while the products with a lower fidelity index should pay higher rates. However, this is not always what happens. Some retailers argue that requesting money for promotional space is a sensible way to ensure that their valuable spaces are used in an efficient manner. Naturally, manufacturers may see such a request as extortion. Many stores are turning their space into real estate, a practice that very much bothers the suppliers who are unable to use their promotional budgets to promote and use them only to "put" their products on good places in the store. There's a phrase that explains the retail-supplier relationship well: "The supplier wants the consumer to buy his product no matter where, and the retailer wants the consumer to buy in his store, no matter what."

How to Improve Promotional Actions

Industry and retail still need to seek common interests. They need to discuss promotions so there will be an investment by and a good result for both sectors. For now, the companies pay and the retailers do not take proper advantage of the arrangement. During "agreed" promotions, retailers don't always respect the contracted spaces and periods, causing damage to the industry. In retail, there tends to be a lack of coordination between the central office and individual stores. Something is agreed upon between the industry and central purchasing, and store management either does not want to comply or wants to do things differently. Retailers should take responsibility and fulfill the agreed-upon commitments.

CHAPTER 6: UNDERSTANDING CUSTOMER PERCEPTION

The idea that brands are made by advertising alone is misguided. Most of the products we put in our shopping carts are brands that have never done advertising but that we admire because of their tradition of quality and competence. It is at the point of purchase where the entire branding strategy is concluded; that's where the brand, after being seen and picked up by the consumer, consolidates and grows, with or without advertising.

Advertising is fundamental to spreading a brand or concept more quickly, but it is not the only thing that needs to be done in a marketing campaign. The entire campaign must be divided between the media and the POP, where the purchasing decision will be made.

Suppliers and retailers must build the brand image of their products, fully aware of the importance of a brand's identity and its ability to retain customers. According to David A. Aaker, recognized as one of the main authorities in the world of brand management, "a successful company, before selling products, sells brands."

In increasingly competitive and sophisticated markets, a portfolio formed by strong brands is a company's most valuable asset. Yet because a strong brand depends on what the consumer believes to be true about it, a brand is nothing more than a set of perceptions.

Memory

Remembrance is important, as people tend to buy well-known brands because they feel comfortable with what is familiar to them. An unknown brand, in contrast, usually has little chance of being considered a viable buying alternative.

Understanding

A consumer's basic understanding of a brand encompasses a series of concepts, all directly influencing the decision to purchase: perceived quality, brand leadership and popularity, perceived value for the money, and brand personality and differentiation.

Loyalty

Loyalty is a brand's ability to attract and keep customers. It is vital to sustaining the brand, because it is more expensive to win new users for any product than to keep existing ones. It also reduces the brand's vulnerability to competitors' actions and implies the possibility of working the best deals within the distribution network.

Brand equity is nothing more than the end result of a set of marketing actions and communications promoting a brand. The more planned and disciplined the brand management, the greater the chance of achieving brand equity: the ideal level of remembrance, understanding, and loyalty.

Brand Identity

Brand identity is what a company wants its brand to mean to the consumer. Every brand must have a unique, distinct, and clearly defined identity.

Brand Experience

From the point of view of the consumer, a brand is the sum total of experiences. It is built incrementally, with each contact between brand and customer, and the POP is the most obvious point of contact.

One of the most important objectives to be considered in the development of any brand marketing program is to ensure that in all promotional activities, everyone in the marketing chain will be speaking with a single voice. All appearances of the brand should be coordinated and express the same identity. Every time and in every situation, those representing the brand need to present a coherent and consistent message. This principle must guide all activities of trade marketing, especially at the POP, which offers the most concrete expression of brand identity.

The Brand and the POP: A Two-Way Street

A portfolio of strong brands is a great facilitator of sales; people tend to buy well-known brands and remain faithful to them because of their quality and perceived value, and because buyers have an emotional connection to them. Still, the merchandising actions at the POP are indispensable to the process of building a brand.

The brand and the POP form a two-way street: the brand helps the store sell, and the selling environment—if well operated—strengthens the brand.

Visual Perception

Visual perception is the principle focus of any marketing effort to promote a brand. The aim is to understand the perception of consumers when they are walking through the aisles of a retail store and to draw a profile of the retailer's capacity to influence them with visual resources. It's important to evaluate how consumers distinguish products and services that lead them to purchase at the POP. That means understanding the stimuli and the situational context that makes a consumer assign quality to a particular product. The quality of a product is the consumer's judgment of it based on clues like brand, price, physical appearance, reputation, packaging, promotional material, and ingredients or components.

Consumers can't remember or categorize as advertisements everything they see in magazines, on billboards, on television, and in other marketing messages. Because of the multiplicity of these messages and interference by other communications, consumers can only remember fragments of information about any particular product. Therefore, all this information must be integrated to avoid cognitive conflict, difficulty in understanding, and consequent rejection.

P. D. Martineau, cited by Christiane Gade (1998), says that, in fact, all products are similar, and so if a product is to be perceived as "unique" and attract brand loyalty, the fundamental point is to establish a differentiated image of the product so that the consumer can easily identify it among the competition. The packaging and the colors of the product help to establish this image.

The marketing creator should seek a motivating, interesting, and original design to catch the prolonged attention of the customer who sees it. This will cause greater interest in the product's message and will allow the customer to think about what the product offers and decide whether to buy it. This technique of contrasting—i.e., the difference between the usual and the unusual that is offered to the senses—is the true invitation that predisposes consumers to understand the marketing message. Their attention, awakened involuntarily, becomes voluntary. It is the extension of attention, motivation, and impact.

We should not forget that good harmony in the design will always prevent attention fatigue. People cannot see and distinguish many visual details at the same time, and so it is advisable to design promotional items with an average of three motivational details, because five or six will disperse the shopper's attention. With fewer details, it is easy to create a center of attention. The continuity and unity of these details must be a fundamental part in an advertising piece because they will keep consumers' attention; otherwise consumers may grow tired and, consequently, disinterested.

It's also important to remember that in a POP gondola, the visual details of one product will be competing with those of hundreds of its nearby competitors, dividing the attention of the individual shopper. Therefore, investments in packaging, brand, a simple name, displays, and support materials are actually investments in capturing customers' attention, shaping their perception, and inspiring them to buy a product at the POP.

Consumer Vision

In sight, in mind.

Vision is the sense responsible for the first step in the purchasing process, because it is the first stimulus that makes the brain react to a particular product. Merchandising creates this first impression, which is very important, because it is at the time of the purchase that the consumer will decide whether to buy your product or your competitor's.

> *The first great challenge of merchandising is to stop consumers and win a few seconds of their attention on the product.*

Scanning Shelves in Seconds

We know that a person's attention is normally fixed on any particular object for two to ten seconds. During the purchasing process, it takes an average of five seconds for a consumer stopped in front of the gondola to make a decision—taking into account that this happens when the consumer is moving, pushing a shopping cart. Between the stops of the shopping cart in locations where the consumer might be interested, the consumer searches with the eyes, scanning shelves, products, brands, and price tags, all within fifteen seconds. If during this time, another package, label, price, or piece of promotional material draws the customer's attention, the customer will spend a few more seconds to make comparisons before choosing the final product.

Practice in choosing and buying might accelerate this process, but it is the consumer's vision—or, better, the consumer's visual perception—that will determine the product to be purchased. The brain, driven by vision, sends the hand to the right product in a matter of seconds.

Memorization and Generalization

Generalization allows consumers to make appropriate and stable responses in life situations without having to formulate a new response every time. Stereotyping is a good example of generalization. If consumers go to a store and verify that its prices are low, they will generalize this expectation for all branches of that store; thus they formed a stereotype according to the similarity among stores. The experience that we have with products and brands involves what is known in marketing as brand generalization. If we like a certain perfume or soap, we expect to like the talc, deodorant, etc., of the same brand.

Certain characteristics generate concepts for better remembrance:
1. a rich and suggestive name
2. an impactful logo
3. the use of colors that draw the attention
4. differentiated and practical packaging
5. a symbol that generates association with the brand
6. text or a slogan that reinforces an idea
7. a song that produces feelings of nostalgia and joy

Another fundamental aspect of memorization is association. The law of association tells us that if we link one idea to another at any point, then from that point on, if we remember the first idea, we'll remember the second one.

In advertising, this principle is used when the names or campaigns for products are created; the product name is associated with the use or usefulness of the product. This strategy is based on the premise that if consumers later realize they need a certain type of product, the product name will come to their minds automatically.

Brands with simple, short, descriptive, meaningful names will be remembered most easily. Those who analyze consumer behavior like to study how a certain brand name is processed and perceived in terms of consumer memory; to what extent that name is learned, retained, and stored in the memory; and what its position is in the consumer's mind.

What is in the shopper's mind—or what's "top of mind" for consumers—has been the focus of extensive research. Therefore with all advertising, psychology comes into play, focused mainly on the process of attention. An advertisement is designed to draw the attention of an individual who reads, listens to, or sees it, thereby completing the selling proposition, which results in a possible purchase. The advertisement creator must make this process happen quickly and unintentionally.

The most important thing is to have direct communication with consumers, catching their attention unexpectedly with a motivational detail such as a certain color or message, which becomes fixed in the mind as quickly as possible.

However, memorizing a brand, a product, or its advertising does not necessarily mean buying the product. There are advertising campaigns that our grandparents still remember today, but unfortunately, the products involved were failures. For this reason, it is necessary to coordinate the advertising campaign with the POP merchandising to seal the purchase. It's not worth winning a Golden Lion Award in Cannes if the client goes bankrupt in the end.

Product Positioning

In marketing, according to Ries and Trout (cited by Gade 1998), consumer perception depends on the best relative position of a product. Thus, marketing is not a battle of products but a battle of perceptions. The image of a product or brand results from symbolic meanings perceived by the consumer, who assigns them to the brand or product. Product placement puts a brand or product in a position relative to the others. Brand identity is the company's vision of it, brand personality is manifested in its physical aspects, and brand image refers to the perception of the consumer. Brand positioning is the final result of the information process. It will determine placement within a product category.

The Perception of Product Brand and Store Brand

It is important to understand the value of brands. A brand only reaches its peak after years of investment in quality and communication, and years of continuous use and approval by consumers.

Packaging—the logos, brands, promotional materials, and displays—carries a brand and reinforces the perceptions of the buyer.

The way a product is presented and displayed in a gondola influences shoppers' visual options. If the product is positioned at eye level and within easy reach, and if there is any promotional appeal, certainly it will be considered an advantageous choice for the consumer.

If consumers don't see a product at the crucial moment of choice, they will forget about it or consider it missing. Worse, if consumers don't see the product, they will buy the competitor's product or switch stores. In self-service, a product not seen is a product not purchased.

Every famous store is associated with a certain color; even children too young to read can see the identifying colors in a storefront or sign and recognize the store. Once when I was riding in the car with my two-year-old daughter, I asked her what that big yellow thing ahead was (the *M* from McDonald's). Her response was "Fries, Mom!" Even foreigners and illiterate adults routinely identify stores by the color and design of their signs or storefronts.

The same occurs when shoppers make purchases at the gondolas. When they see a product, the first thing they "read" on the packaging is the color, even before they read the label or logo. After the colors, they "read" any image or figure on the packaging. Only after that do they read the logo or big print (forget about the small print). That's why some companies copy the famous packaging of their competitors.

When people buy what they think they already know, they pick up the product as quickly as they can. As a result, many of them never read the secondary information on the package.

Packaging

Packaging and the Decision-Making Process

Packaging has a power of attraction and fascination that acts directly on human senses. It reaches the motivational part of the brain that leads the individual to sate an impulsive desire by making a purchase.

Packaging is no longer just a protective enclosure for a product or the element that facilitates its distribution. To these functions were added others that require attention and care on part of the technicians who are concerned with its design.

Product identification in the market is not a function of brand alone. Packaging—including shape, color, and text—is also a discriminating factor. Besides being a direct and active advertising vehicle, a package can suggest the level of quality of its contents. Consumers' perception of packaging is an exciting force that can compel them to purchase the packaged product. A complex process begins the moment a consumer is excited by a displayed object and ends when the consumer acquires that object. Reason doesn't enter the process, although the individual is always ready to rationalize the purchase. However, we must not forget the groundwork laid by advertising, which prepared the consumer's subconscious mind, ultimately facilitating the choice.

The full unity of all the details that make up a product's packaging should inspire confidence in shoppers and inspire mental associations that are likely to lead them to purchase it.

Packaging Visibility

From the point of view of sales, having visibility means making the product stand out among a multitude of other displayed products.

The main function of packaging is to cause the sale of the product. That means it must have characteristics that suggest the product's use, and it must have strong visibility, because consumers walking through the store aisles with the intention of acquiring a specific product will stop many times along the way to look at other products that catch their attention.

Important questions that merchandising and packaging design professionals must consider:
1. Can the product or brand be identified immediately from four meters away?
2. Does the packaging clearly reflect the product's use or purpose?
3. Will customers quickly understand what the product does? (Is there clarity of presentation/message?)
4. Does the packaging attract the eye when placed among competitors on the shelves?
5. If the product is mountable, electrical, mechanical, or electronic, does it have enough specifications on the packaging (voltage, capacity, power, etc.) for a customer to make the quick decision to buy it?
6. Do several packages together create a larger image? Is the effect pleasing or confusing?
7. Is the packaging sized appropriately for the gondolas or displays in many types of stores?
8. Was the packaging factory-tested to ensure that it will protect the product and maintain its quality?
9. Is the packaging material resistant to customer use of or contact with the product (is it plasticized, etc.)?
10. Is the product legally approved, with visible stamps / government seals / quality certificates?
11. Is the product's brand or design registered?

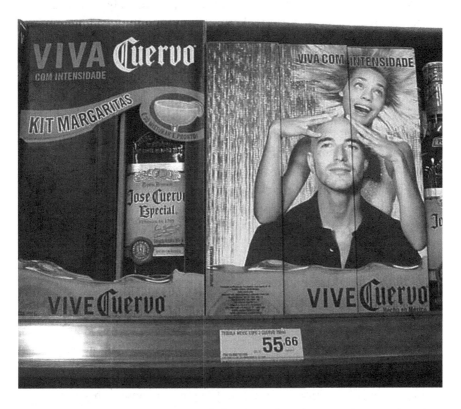

Packaging with a well-planned design makes the complete product line a real billboard inside the store. No matter how bad the merchandiser is, the effect will always be beautiful.

Note: I hate to talk about colors in a black-and-white book. But I've posted photos in full color on my website, www.no-failretail.com, so you can see examples of effective and ineffective uses of color in packaging.

Packaging has the magical function of calling to the consumer. A package's color is what gets the first look; therefore it should be the designer's first concern, especially considering the emotional connections involved with color and its great suggestive and persuasive power. The presence of color in packaging is of unquestioned value.

There is no doubt that the positioning and arrangement of packages in a window or on store shelves have an important function here, too. A product that is closer to shoppers allows them to see its design and interesting graphic details, and read the text on the packaging.

When designers create a line of packages in the same category, the larger packages should be the same size as multiples of the smaller ones to facilitate arrangement on the shelves. Very small products should be placed in blister packs that will facilitate their display and reduce theft, otherwise they will be lost behind a counter.

Every advertiser knows that the most important aspect of packaging is its motivational appeal, because you don't sell a product, you sell an idea—a way to satisfy a desire or fulfill a need.

Consumers' and dealers' expectations about product packaging should not discourage marketing executives in their search for innovation. But frequent changes in packaging dimensions or designs can make some consumers resistant to buying, especially when the configuration of existing shelves does not lend itself to easily accommodate the new packaging.

Every time a marketing team needs packaging for their product but does not ask for collaboration of the merchandising team, they will just be creating one more package, not the appropriate one for displaying at the shelves.

Even with an ongoing campaign, cyclically, the products require a small shove to jump from the gondolas to the buyer's cart in the store.

(Based on Gade, Psicologia do Consumidor e da Propaganda)

The Challenge of Attracting the Consumer

Currently, one of the biggest challenges that the market faces is the vast accumulation of commercial information and advertising messages that the consumer receives every day. Some experts in communication and marketing have estimated that consumers receive more than three thousand promotional messages daily.

This wealth of information causes some problems for retailers, whose messages get lost when they display products and brands for their customers, or when they organize and create advertising pieces to promote special offers in order to achieve their merchandising goals.

Integrated marketing communication proposes that companies learn to use communication tools—advertising, sales promotions, public relations, merchandising, direct marketing—in a more effective and efficient way. To this end, they should promote several actions, speaking to different audiences to which they relate, such as employees, suppliers, investors, opinion formers, and consumers in general, generating selective attention in order to occupy a positive space in shoppers' minds. A memorable brand, a desirable product, and a good public image within the community become the major marketing objective. These are the fundamental factors that will continue to help sell more products.

The importance of branding, technological improvements in the production and distribution of products and services, and the increasing use of integrated communication have led companies, mainly in the retail sector, to return to the consumer experience with products. Today, with the great diversity of products available and the excessive amount of advertising aimed at consumers, marketers must regard the consumer's decision-making process as the key to solving a product's sales problems and prolonging that product's existence in the market.

CHAPTER 7:
CUSTOMER CARE

Have you ever been poorly treated in a store? If so, did you return there to buy again?

Customer Service

The competition for excellence in customer service is constant in more advanced world markets. Millions of dollars are spent on customer service, and that investment is returned in customer interest, dividends, and company image. Then again, the concept of customer service is almost nonexistent in some countries. It seems that some traders are not interested in pleasing consumers.

Customer service begins with the seller. It is up to the seller to communicate with consumers, to inform them about delivery problems, to confirm the receipt of desired products, or to follow up after a sale to make sure everything is going well.

Post-sale service is indispensable, because it transforms the sporadic buyer into a permanent consumer. On-site assistance is also important. Try to call a store manager on the phone. As a rule he is never there, or if he is, he won't take your call. His staff might tell you that he went somewhere and will return soon, but the reality is that he is never around.

Some stores or services have a consumer complaint service, but often it is useless, as there is never anyone with enough authority to solve your problem. Only the manager or someone in a higher position—that is, someone who is never available—can solve it. In this case, we recommend improving your customer service.

There is not a more hypocritical statement than "Your call is very important to us." If that statement were true, nobody would have to listen to it twenty times while waiting on hold.

Since the advent of the Internet, many stores handle customer service exclusively through their websites. Some do not even post a physical address or a phone number, leaving consumers terrified. With nowhere to turn for assistance, many consumers give up before even buying.

Word of Mouth and Negative Image

Every consumer who is well served talks with five other people about his or her satisfaction. Every consumer who is poorly served complains—loudly—to fifteen others about his or her disappointment. The negative publicity transmitted from person to person can be more devastating than any action by a company's competitors.

Imagine this sort of negative publicity happening in geometric progression—in a family, then a street, then a neighborhood ... Mistakes happen in retail, but a lot of them can compromise the future of a store. It is up to the owner or manager to learn what really matters to the consumer and teach employees the right way to handle mistakes.

The large stores inside malls typically disregard their customers because their traffic flow is rich and varied. Since the source of the flow is never exhausted, these retailers do not pay much attention to customer service; their primary consideration is momentary market factors. In contrast, a neighborhood store very much depends on its image in the neighborhood or region where it operates. It can never ignore a drop in its popularity and should continually seek excellence in its customer care, products and services, and price. Even stores in good locations can close if they drive away their consumers through incompetence. The first lesson to be learned, then, is that the customer is the boss. It's the customer, along with his or her friends, relatives, and community, who have the power to close a business.

How to Enchant the Consumer

There are eight basic rules for achieving excellence in customer service:

1. The example must come from the top.
Participation by the company's president and chief executives is vital. They should leave their domes and commit themselves personally to the customers, visiting them regularly, answering their calls, and responding to their letters or e-mails.

2. Everybody needs to be involved.

Customer service cannot be allocated to a specific sector of the company. From the janitor to the office worker to the telephone operator, everyone must participate in and feel responsible for pleasing the customer. Make sure that the company's recruitment practices, training, and recycling also support that goal.

3. Delegate authority in customer service.

At a critical moment, the customer cannot wait for decisions to be made at the highest level. They should be made by someone who is on the front lines.

4. The customer service department must deliver fast service.

The department should prioritize complaints so that the most serious ones are answered in twenty-four hours or less.

5. Always listen to the customer.

Customers' aspirations and desires change constantly. What is good today may not be good tomorrow. Periodic surveys or staff meetings can help companies fine-tune service policies and provide guidance for the required adjustments.

6. Work in partnership with customers.

The retailer's relationship with the customer does not end with a simple sale. Retailers must be prepared to offer assistance about the best way to use its product or service.

7. Change the criteria for evaluating employees.

In an analysis of employee performance and potential remuneration, high customer satisfaction should be as important as increased market share or sales. Every customer should be treated as unique.

8. Invest in training.

Training for client satisfaction often requires a big cultural change in a company. For this reason, it is necessary to train employees in the concepts of total quality and in the techniques of human relations. No company is a "ten" if its staff is a "five."

Customer-Centric Retailing

To administrate a store does not just mean standing behind the counter and ringing up sales. It is also not enough just to offer products. Having a store means stimulating purchases and exposing the public to the latest news in the market.

It is possible to know a good store by observing its entry, its product displays, the demeanor of its clerks, the distribution of its display space, and, finally, the quality of its service. The store space must be optimized without forgetting the principles of good management; to retain customers, a store must take the best advantage of product displays while still having a pleasant ambiance.

What image does your store convey? This question is crucial, and it should be analyzed with all sincerity, because in a store, everything "speaks": the employees; the store's cleanliness, décor, and use of space; and its offerings and promotional materials. The exploitation of windows, shelves, promotion spots, and aisles to concentrate the flow of customers, causing the formation of lines, are problems that should be observed and remedied through good merchandising.

Merchandising is the application of sales promotions and display techniques generated by manufacturers, distributors, or stores. It requires placing the products correctly: in the proper position, in the proper season, and in a quantity and at a price that enables customers to find a particular product easily, in favorable conditions.

Here is how to create the impression that a company's products and services are unique.

First Impressions Are the Most Lasting

A customer's first contact with a store is the most important, because that may be what determines whether the customer enters, buys, gives up, or goes back.

When you stand on the sidewalk and look inside a store, you make a quick assessment of three things:
- what the store sells
- the store's standards and quality
- the demeanor of the sales staff

From there, you will make a decision. If you have an urgent need for something, you'll go and try it even if you do not like the store. If your need is not urgent and you don't like what you see from the sidewalk, you'll go to another store. Once inside the store, you'll look for the product category. If you see the product on the shelf, you'll ask for it so you can feel it, check its price, and decide whether or not to purchase it. If you don't find the product category, you'll begin looking for something that might serve the purpose, and choose the product that seems best.

For stores, the first impression can come from some direct channels of communication with their consumers, including the following:

- store website
- store telephone
- in-store personnel
- home delivery courier

You can also speak with customers indirectly, through advertising. A store's image in the media is usually prepared by creative hands who always manage to project a positive and happy picture of excited buyers who want to go to the store. It is clear that the actors who appear in the ads do not actually work in the store, meeting the demands of consumers. In an advertisement, everything is beautiful and perfect—it's an unreal world. In the real world, a store needs to be close to its advertised standards so that it can deliver what was promised in the media.

Learn Which Customers Should Receive Special Treatment

Positioning a store well means offering a certain value—whether through the type or quality of its service—that highlights the difference between the store and its competitors.

The priorities of a traditional store should include modernization, improving the orientation of the product to the customer, and maintaining a team that is well trained and that is oriented to the shopper, not itself.

In achieving those priorities, one of the steps retailers must not forget is the team analysis, since the human resource is one of the main factors in retail that must be controlled. In fact, it may be the most important factor, since humans are the key to providing proper attention to the customer. A proper analysis is performed through surveys, personal interviews, studies of the organization, and an assessment of the attitudes and skills of the owner. The objective is to prove that the store has the appropriate number of employees, the correct level of professionalism, a good incentive plan, and the best possible leader.

The retailer must achieve fluidity and understanding among the employees by holding meetings at least once a month to motivate them, share goals, raise issues, and keep the team informed and participative in terms of both concrete actions and upholding the general philosophy of the store.

Above all, good customer service means providing quality care and a good level of products and services; carrying out promotions; creating customer databases; offering prizes, differentiated services, or special promotions; offering samples, giveaways, or birthday discounts; and monitoring the results. All these factors contribute to customer loyalty and store positioning.

Know Your Audience

Information is the basic tool of marketing for any business.

To ensure that a retailer earns the loyalty of consumers, it needs to know who those customers are: where they live, how much they earn, how much they spend, where else they shop, whether they drive or walk, whether they are satisfied with the store's services and customer care, etc.

There are many organizations that collect data, but few use it properly. Knowing how to leverage customer/consumer data should be the purview of an entire department in a chain of stores. Credit card transactions, checks received, funding and promotional deals that involve filling out store questionnaires—all these elements generate customer data that can be very helpful in assessing the pattern of consumption in a store.

Women's Buying Power

Buying power is defined as the total personal income that is available, after taxes, for spending on virtually anything, including goods and services. It is also called disposable income.

In general, buying power is challenging to measure, particularly the buying power of women. Both Canadian and US census income data are reported by household unit. Since about half of women are married householders, their individual spending is lost in the "household" spending, and thus difficult to isolate. The finding that most women are the "principal shoppers" in their households implies that women make the majority of household purchases or decisions to make household purchases, but there is little concrete data associated with that implication. Census findings do imply that spending increases with income, so a case can be made that as women's incomes increase, so does their spending. By combining statistics below, some evidence for both trends is supported.

Women Make Key Purchasing Decisions

- According to MRI's Survey of the American Consumer, 74.9 percent of women identified themselves as the primary shoppers for their households.
- According to a study from the Boston Consulting Group, women in the US reported "controlling" 72.8 percent of household spending, and women in Canada reported "controlling" 67.2 percent of household spending. Additionally, women "control $12 trillion of the overall $18.4 trillion in global consumer spending." The survey actually asked whether women "controlled or influenced" purchases, which is much a broader distinction.

(Catalyst. Catalyst Quick Take: Buying Power.)

Employees versus Consumer

It is rare to find a consumer who has not been upset during some commercial transaction. All of us are consumers in various types of POPs. Try to put yourself in the place of your customers during shopping, and monitor the remarks, attitudes, and expressions of the consumers who shop in your store. Do they seem angry or relaxed and happy? Do they smile at the clerks or glare at them? You can learn a lot this way. There are store managers who assess their employees based only on the number of complaints they receive, but those managers forget that only one percent of consumers actually take the time to complain when they're unhappy. Look for yourself and draw your own conclusions quickly, before it's too late.

Contact with People

Over the years, we observed that there is a strong correlation between the high staff turnover and the low level of satisfaction on the part of consumers, so we have to pay attention when recruiting associates that will attend our customers.

When we recruit people for positions inside an office, the ability to serve the customers is not as worthy as the empathy towards the team. But when we recruit people for positions where they will meet our shoppers, our responsibility is much greater. These workers' appearance, their ability to communicate, their promptness, their level of knowledge, their diplomatic skills, and their natural patience with the public all matter very much.

Do not simply go after beauty; there are lots of beautiful but unsympathetic people. Instead, seek people with good looks who are also super-friendly. And always choose smiling candidates. A smile is worth a lot when it comes to winning customers.

Explain to your employees that both physical appearance and a good attitude are fundamental to winning consumers. And keep in mind that it is best to select your employees well than to spend all day asking your "cute" employee to make a better face.

Promotional Work Force

A merchandiser is the person who ensures that products and promotional items are in the right place at the right time, in the right quantity, and of the right quality. All the merchandising work done inside the POP has immediate ramifications on product sales and the retailer's business performance. Good merchandising results in better product turnover and encourages consumers to buy more. On the other hand, poor merchandising can drag down sales, resulting in the failure of a store or of a product on the market.

Stockers, demonstrators, promoters, and merchandisers in the POP should be carefully trained and managed to know how to advance the store's goals and sell its products to customers every day. This specialized work force is highly valued by retailers, who are already aware of the fact that such a team delivers only very real advantages:

- It increases average sales.
- It attracts more customers to the store.
- It improves customer loyalty and increases store profits.

Benefits to Retailers

Merchandisers, demonstrators, and stockers may provide other benefits to retailers, as well, including the following:

- savings with work force
- fewer product shortages, resulting in fewer lost sales
- better-highlighted products, resulting in increased sales
- correct placement of promotional material
- help with pricing and detection of incorrectly marked prices
- avoid sales of expired products
- accelerated exchange of damaged products by the manufacturer
- merchandising training for beginning stockers
- instruction to other store employees about product function
- control missing quality seals, in order to avoid tax assessments
- access to market information about the entire category of products
- better communication between the store and its suppliers

Personal Profile for the POP Worker

Workers in the POP should have the following characteristics:

- good physical appearance
- a constant smile and friendly attitude
- a lively demeanor and straight posture
- a white, healthy-looking smile
- a clear, friendly tone of voice and polite language (no slang)
- a hygienic appearance, a fresh smell, and clean, trimmed nails
- clean hair and tied back (if worker is dealing with food)
- simple, natural-looking makeup
- modest jewelry
- clean uniforms that are not clingy or baggy; skirts should be medium-length
- no smoking or chewing gum in the store

The work of stockers, demonstrators, promoters, and merchandisers should be highly valued by retailers. These workers are on the front lines of retail, where brands and stores fight to win customers.

Functions of Merchandisers

The professionals who work in the POP are responsible for the following functions:

- cleaning the products and the shelves around them
- opening boxes to expose the products
- placing the products in the best location on the gondola
- increasing the fronts (spaces) intended for each product
- maximizing the available space
- seeking extra spots in the store where they can put more merchandise
- making piles and islands
- constantly refilling shelves, piles, islands, displays, and materials
- arranging products for better visualization
- placing promotional material in a manner that respects the layout of the store
- not interfering with the duties of store employees
- switching out unusable or expired products
- organizing and replenishing warehoused merchandise
- staying alert to the activities of competitors
- when asked, providing information about products to retailers and consumers
- informing the company about competitors (day-to-day problems, prices, other news)
- informing retailers about the performance of their products
- noting how consumers react to the products
- following the life of products in the sales area and the warehouse

Checklist for Professional Skills Training

Workers in the POP should possess or be trained in the following professional skills:

- proven experience or intensive training in service
- knowledge of the products and their origins
- knowledge of the competition, with the understanding that undermining the competition is unethical
- knowledge of how to use the equipment and/or adequately handle the products

- the ability to politely greet approaching customers
- the understanding that it is never acceptable to look away from or fail to serve a customer
- the ability to listen to customers and answer them promptly
- the ability to circumvent objections about the products
- the understanding that it is never acceptable to prejudge customers by their appearance or otherwise show prejudice
- the ability to acknowledge and apologize for failures
- knowledge of the proper treatment of fellow workers

Technology has contributed to the cost reduction and increased productivity in retail. The use of new tools, such as RFID, smart phones, tablets and many other friendly technologies that appear daily, helps the team of merchandisers and sales associates to capture accurately and quickly the data of the stores as price, ruptures, real and virtual inventory, competition, promotional actions and other information with photos in real-time control of everything. These are weapons that give a strategic advantage both for retailers and for industries.

CHAPTER 8:
THE POINT OF PURCHASE AS MEDIA

All types of signs inform, remind, persuade, indicate position, expose, and sell. A product that is not well displayed is not seen. A product that is not seen is not purchased. The material at the point of purchase is what gives voice to the product, saying, "Hey! I'm here!"

The POP is a measurable media, like any other vehicle of communication, but it has a more important function, because it combines the location where the product is decided and chosen and the exact time of purchase.

Marketing and advertising plan to create brands and strengthen products cannot exclude the work done with in-store materials— that is, materials designed to create an impact on the consumer inside the POP. These promotional materials don't just influence consumers who remember advertising and buy; and also dispense and encourage the purchase of other, similar products that were not the subject of any promotion.

In addition to helping with the positioning and display of products, POP materials are the main tool of an advertising campaign to complement the purchasing desire it creates. POP media should be consider and recognized as advertising especially for dangerous products as tobacco and alcohol.

For example, point of purchase tobacco displays, or tobacco "power walls", are the most important advertising medium available to the tobacco industry. Arguably, this is the reason why tobacco companies spend billions with in-store advertising. The tobacco product displays are very effective for adults, but they also reach and influence children and teens inside the stores and as advertising should be banned.

In-store media can include bright internal promotional spaces; signs on gondolas or on the tops of gondolas; internal backlights; totems; inflatables; and indicator signs in the parking lot, among other items that can be rented or provided by the store.

There is an infinite number of merchandising technologies and materials for the POP, and new creative pieces are appearing each day.

Promotional Material

The communication or information on any promotional material should be simple and straightforward. Because of the environment into which it is inserted, where thousands of brands and packages are vying for customers' attention, the material must have vibrant or contrasting colors, and its text should be brief, with large, easy-to-read letters, if customers are going to notice and remember it.

Every day new types of promotional materials appear. The most common are displays, posters, flags, indicators, panels, exhibit booths, signs, shelves blades, and ceiling mobiles. All in-store materials should comply with the following basic criteria to achieve maximum effectiveness:

- They should be placed in areas of greater traffic flow.
- They must avoid any conflict between the displayed product and the advertised product.
- They should be placed where they can be seen (at the proper visual angle), never lower than customers' knees or higher than their heads.

How to Create Good In-Store Material

Just as a product's promotional materials must complement its advertising, they also must fit into the store's promotional scheme. Here are some general rules to keep in mind:

- Creativity: The in-store material must be creative and dimensionally proportionate to the location where it will be applied (e.g., shelf, end cap, wall, checkout, ceiling or floor).
- Originality: A clever design, an appropriate theme, short and easy-to-read text, and good visual impact will make customers remember the message.
- Functionality: Simplicity; good accommodation of the product; easy assembly, positioning, and easy replacement will ensure the material's acceptance and use by retailers.

Basic Criteria for Obtaining Maximum Efficiency with the POP

Before promotional materials for the POP are created, several questions need to be answered:
- What are the primary objectives of the project?
- What are the placement possibilities of the material in the retail environment?
- What are the possibilities for displaying the product inside or outside the shelves?
- What are the size requirements for the material?
- What is the target number of POPs for the material?
- Who are the target user and shopper for this project?
- How long will the material or display be in the field?

After the project is well analyzed and defined, the materials should be planned based on the following guidelines:
- The size and type of materials should be appropriate for the POP.
- Proper accommodations should be made for electric or hydraulic installation or support.
- Materials should be placed in areas of greater customer flow.
- Materials should be easy to pack, ship, and mount.
- Materials should stay where they can be seen (at the appropriate visual angle).
- Materials should be displayed so they are accessible without hindering customers' handling of the products.

Here are a few more tips:
- Never make the shelf material the same colors as the packaged products behind it, because the shelf material will disappear. This is a common mistake made by advertising agencies. All materials should contrast so they can be easily read.
- All materials should leave space for the price; otherwise they will not be used by the store.
- The shelf materials (wobblers, stoppers, danglers, etc.) should never hide important parts of the product package, like the name or brand. To avoid this other common

mistake, always check the layout beforehand in a real store, and not just on a computer screen.
- Pay attention to legibility. Any sign or promotional material should be readable from three meters away.

Advantages of Materials

The materials at the POP usually reinforce the advertising message consumers have seen before entering the store. In general, merchandising materials expand the effects of advertising, because they complement its messages directly in the store where purchasing decisions are made.

However, for suppliers who do not have the means to advertise in print or electronic media, in-store materials are the most reasonable alternative, for two reasons:

First, POP programs focus on the consumer and the marketing of merchandise at a crucial moment: the time of purchase. Because effective POP materials make merchandise go from the shelves to the hands of the consumer, the investment in their production is quickly justified. Store cash registers can generate immediate sales data that both the manufacturer and the retailer can use to evaluate the impact of materials or programs.

Second, POP programs are a good example of flexible marketing. They can easily be drawn up according to local market needs, chains, or specific trades. In addition, they allow suppliers to target certain types of consumers in specific stores.

Impact of Materials

Almost all stores use promotional materials, however, it is also known that their index of perception by customers does not reach 30 percent.

There are many factors that negatively affect the perception of materials. Here are the most common ones:
- a poor arrangement
- material that's the same color as the product underneath it (generally wobblers)
- a hidden section
- a display position below knee level
- an excess of materials in the area

Here are the materials that are known to work better:
* special price tags
* price offer posters or promotions
* wobblers and stoppers
* shelf talker blades
* flags
* islands
* hanging ceiling mobiles (for low ceilings)
* floor stickers
* leaflets / take one display
* clip strips
* cardboard display for endcaps (photo)

An image speaks more than a thousand words.

Types of Displays and Their Uses

Promotional materials are separated into three categories: permanent, semipermanent, and temporary.

Permanent materials are specially produced to complement specific store spaces or create extra spots. In general, they are made of wire, steel, masonry, glass, acrylic, resin, or some other material sturdy enough to last at least one year in the store.

Semipermanent materials are those that stay approximately six months in the store for a long promotion or product support. They can be made of cardboard, wood, steel, wire, etc. Their appearance is temporary, but they are durable enough to stay in use far longer than a few weeks.

Temporary (or disposable) materials are displayed for just a few weeks, long enough to support any promotion or advertising campaign. They are usually made of cardboard or plastic and have a short life.

It is estimated that 40 percent of the promotional materials sent to POPs do not reach their destination, the area of sale. This merchandising disaster is in part the result of the disinterest of retailers, who receive many such materials and often are not concerned with whatever investment an industry might have made to get them to sell more. But the other part of the problem is that supplier companies with little experience in POP send off their displays to stores in distant cities without even an assembly manual. As self-assembling displays have not been invented yet, someone has to follow up and send a team to provide that service.

All communication must be recent. Old ones left over on displays of new products give the impression of sloppiness, and signs that are forgotten or worn harm the image of the store.

In each of the above three categories, there are several types of displays:

Floor Displays

These are all the large displays, aside from gondolas, that stand on the floor. A floor display should be big enough to stay beside an endcap without disturbing the flow of customers. Floor displays are recommended only for stores that have extra space.

Counter Displays

These are displays used as extra spots on the counter. Because they should be small and contain few items, they require greater attention to refilling.

Shelf Displays

Although these are similar to counter displays, they need be sized to fit on the shelves of supermarkets or stores. They also must be reinforced to withstand self-service (incorrect handling), be easy to refill, and serve consumers well. Some products cannot stand by themselves, so they need a nest display that allows all the products to stand up and offers information about the brand and product features.

Checkout Displays

Because the checkout is a mandatory stop for customers, it leads to high sales and high turnover. This area is not advisable for promotion displays unless the product itself is displayed there. It is an ideal spot for impulse products.

Displays on Endcaps

These displays must be tailor-made after negotiations with and permission from the store, or their assembly must be improvised with whatever parts are available in order to attract attention to the products.

An endcap is the most coveted place to expose a product or a line of products from the same company. For customers, endcaps are synonymous with promotion and low price. The majority of consumers already assume that buying what is on the endcap is advantageous—even when it's not. Therefore, these spaces are usually rented by stores.

Demonstration Counters

This POP material usually comprises a small booth for a demonstrator who aims to show and disseminate a product in a customized way. In general, the booth is easy to disassemble and carry.

Banners

Banners are flags of any size (from small to giant), made of paper, plastic, or fabric. They are inexpensive, very practical for time-sensitive promotions, and ideal for signaling events.

Informational or Promotional Cards and Mini-Brochures

When used as campaign hooks, these materials can influence customers at the time of purchase.

Price Tags

Standard price tags are the store's responsibility; they are mandatory and help consumers understands the terms of purchase. Special price tags with visual emphasis (using colors or some other design splash) can influence customers' purchase decisions.

Shelf Talker Blades

These blades, made of cardboard or plastic, inform customers about the presence of a product on the shelf and help them locate the product among the many others that surround it. They are fitted into transparent strips or glued to the vertical shelf supports. They should be as long as three or four packages and narrow enough not to obscure the brand name or the price tags.

The blades should be made for best visual effect, with colors that contrast with the majority of competitors' packaging, short text with large letters, and a message that reveals the quality of the product.

Shelf talker blades reserve shelf space for and call attention to products.

Door Sign

A door sign is a good inexpensive alternative to catch the attention of people passing by.

It really grabs people's attention when your sign shows one special offer. If you make a sign full of offers, their level of attention will fall drastically. This is an example of an effective sign.

Inflatables

Inflatable plastic displays or promotional balloons can be used to imitate any form, such as product packages. Quite showy when they are large, they help merchandisers decorate for events and promote products or companies inside the store as well as outside, such as in the store parking lot.

Printed Pallet Wraps

Also known as base wrap, pallet wrap is the perfect way to dress up pallets of product or to create store signage in windows or on walls. This easy-to-use product allows for the application of brand graphics to create in-store signs, banners, and more.

Bottleneckers

A bottlenecker is a promotional element placed around the neck of a glass or plastic bottle. As it is attached to the product, it is not considered an extra promotional material and is therefore well accepted by stores.

A bottlenecker is a fantastic material for getting a message home to customers, but tries not to use it to explain the entire promotional campaign.

Hanging Mobile Ceiling Displays

These displays are promotional pieces suspended from the ceiling with strings. They are most often seen in convenience stores, small markets, drugstores, and specialty stores, which tend to have low ceilings.

Hanging displays are best used for images and brands. It's not advisable to use them to convey any information written in small print, because their height and their tendency to blow around make them difficult to read. They must be made with a select few images and large letters.

Product Replicas
These packages are ten times bigger than the original product and can be placed on shelves as promotional displays.

Stickers
These self-adhesive plastic materials containing promotional messages are well accepted in bars, coffee shops, and drugstores, as well as on supermarket freezers and refrigerators. They can be stuck anywhere—some can even be stuck to the store floor—with special, easy-to-clean glue.

Stoppers/Wobblers/Danglers
These are cardboard or plastic flags that fit at the edges of shelves, sticking out sort of like ears. They are very attractive and functional, and if they are designed properly, they can be perceived at a distance by the consumer.

A wobbler has a transparent plastic tongue that moves along with air movement, calling even more attention to the product. There are also stoppers that use LED lights, sound, and even smell.

This stopper is indicating a sale. Great to see it while walking at the aisle.

Flyers, Tabloids, Mailers, Brochures and Store Circulars

To attract consumers, we need to keep high synchrony between the product offered and consumer desire. When they send direct mailings or flyers to consumers in a specific region, they need to evaluate the demographics: the target consumer's profile, needs, and interests. So those traditional promotions, which attracted crowds before, have been replaced by lighter artillery based on consumer research on the region or cluster of consumption reached by a particular store.

Brochure Holders or "Take Ones"

These are open boxes or dispensers placed on shelves or counters so that consumers can take the small brochures or flyers inside.

Be careful with promotional material, which can be easily damaged through mishandling. Do not use heavy papers in a weak box.

Merchandising Strips

Merchandising strips, made from durable plastic or even steel, can be used multiple times thanks to their sturdy construction. These "clip strips" are largely used for cross merchandising.

Interactive Displays

These are compact kiosks or electronic terminals in which the customer gets information, publicity materials, or coupons through a computerized program without the help of a clerk. They can involve multiple media, with a TV set, sound system, computer, etc.

Some products need an explanation or demonstration that it is not always possible to provide.

To promote a product beyond these basic interactive displays, there are displays with videos that introduce the product with a five-second advertisement plus a ten-second explanation, and, if needed, a one-minute description of the finer details. If the video is longer than that, consumers just will not stop to watch it.

Other In-Store Media

There are other special vehicles for advertising or promotion that can be placed inside a store, such as closed-circuit TVs that play commercials, in-store speakers that play special radio programming announcing offers, and videos in endcaps that pass along product information or play commercials. Without a doubt, these media are great channels of communication with consumers inside the store, but they require carefully crafted messaging to grab people's attention between purchases.

Communication with the Consumer

Promotional actions should be planned according to a calendar—annual, semiannual, or quarterly. Each task involved in the promotion should be planned with a specific date in mind, as well as with a specific budget and requisitions for staff training, space, and publicity.

The advertising campaign must maintain consistent messaging, use language suitable for the target audience, and preserve the chain or store image. All these factors will reflect positively on the store brand and bring the appearance of quality to what is being offered.

For a merchandising action to work well, it is important to observe the store from the point of view of the customers that enter and leave it every day. Retailers should analyze customers' reactions to the store environment, noting whether they are entering and buying or simply entering and leaving. Merchandisers should introduce small promotional actions and analyze the results, learning from their errors and not interrupt the consumer impulse with internal barriers. They should make the store environment communicative and exciting, always seeking to surprise the faithful customer.

To achieve these results, it is essential that the supplier gives support by defining a planogram and its expected results, analyzing the promotional material and products, and respecting the overall management of the store space. It should be noted that merchandising is a continuous process that must be regularly updated. When the plan is initiated, both the supplier and the store must establish a system for monitoring it and measuring its results.

If the results are not as expected, it's important to establish a contingency plan with measures to correct the defective points and emphasize the successful ones.

ROI: Return on Investment

An agency specializing in POP can and should inform its clients of all the positive and negative aspects that happen in front of the consumer. What normally happens is that, before a big promotion and before a client or store hires such an agency for the promotion period, the client or store has not saved prior sales data on the product in question. If the store does not know how a product has performed in the months before the promotional action, it loses the comparative reference of before-and-after data. That means any assessment of the promotional action will be based on the gut feelings of the salespeople and the store owner or manager. With comparative information, it is possible to evaluate the impact of merchandising activities on a product, both individually and relative to its product category. The client, the store, and the specialty agency should use sales reports to raise issues that are relevant to the success of the program. Ideally, there should be standard sales reports generated during the four months before the action; surveys (sales and effects) generated during the entire promotional period; and continued reports generated during the four months afterward to evaluate residual market gain.

Shopper Marketing versus In-Store Marketing

Shopper marketing starts outside the store, because that's where shopping starts. However, the majority of shopping decisions (90 to 60 percent, depending on the category) are made at the point of purchase, because this is where many shopping trips start.

Whatever the number is for a particular brand or category, a significant number of a product's target shoppers are making some shopping decisions outside the store. That is, many of them approve or reject a product or brand well before they reach the store entrance.

We've all made decisions at the point of purchase, and we're very conscious of those. Further, so much research focuses on the in-store decision-making process that we sometimes forget that there are other times and places where buying decisions are made. Shopping decisions start as soon as there is an immediate or anticipated need. That first decision is often whether or not to embark upon a purchase path to meet that need. The process of buying varies by shopper, by category, by channel, and even by country, but it is a universal truth that once a consumer decides that a brand really can't help on a particular shopping mission, that brand is out of contention for good.

So marketers must recognize that while there is much to be won or lost in the store, there is plenty to be won or lost outside the store, too. Understanding shoppers' states of mind before they enter the store (too often research focuses only on what happens in-store) helps identify which shoppers already have a positive (or negative) disposition as they enter. With this information, marketers can define clear objectives for the pre-store and in-store marketing mix. Knowing which stores have which shoppers also helps define priorities by channel. Shopper marketers need to work with consumers wherever they can be influenced. For some categories and brands, if they choose to focus on the in-store world only, they run the risk of having lost the battle before they've even begun it.

CHAPTER 9:
THE PSYCHOLOGY OF CONSUMPTION

The behavior of consumption is defined as the behavior of the demand, purchase, use, and evaluation of products or services. It can be described as the physical, mental, and emotional activities involved in selecting, purchasing, and using products or services to the satisfaction of the consumer's needs and desires.

Consumer behavior has been analyzed by professionals in psychology, consumption analysis, advertising, and economics. Their research enables us to better understand the influences of psychodynamic internal factors and psychosocial external factors that act on the consumer's mind. This knowledge has allowed for the development of more effective marketing strategies.

The Economic Theory of Consumption

Humans have infinite needs and desires but finite means to satisfy them. We cannot obtain, purchase, consume, and use whatever we want; we are forced to make choices. During this process of choosing, we tend to maximize our consumption; in other words, considering our limitations, we will tend to choose whatever gives us the maximum pleasure or compensation.

Two positions arise from this truth:
1. that of the individual consumer, who wants to take maximum advantage of what can be consumed and who therefore chooses what seems to be the more profitable option
2. that of the company, which, knowing that the customer can't buy everything, expect that chooses its product.

Humans, in search of pleasure, generate usefulness through their consumption, because by seeking to increase their pleasure and minimize their suffering, they consume merchandise and services that provide them greater utility.

Gauging the value that each individual assigns to a product is a difficult task. The value of a product is what it offers in relation to its price. To one customer, cheese packaged in transparent plastic may be judged less valuable than cheese packaged in a glass container that can be reused later. To another customer, the second product may have less value, because the glass is heavier and can break during transportation. This is an example of how the economic theory of consumer behavior allows for a partial understanding of consumer psychology.

The income factor has great importance in economic theory and makes a big difference in consumer behavior. Statistical data about family spending across several income levels clearly shows that the absolute cost of merchandise purchased increases with income.

While spending on food decreases as a proportion of total spending, and spending on housing and clothing is the same or just slightly higher, spending on luxuries grows in proportion to income. With higher income comes a craving for more luxuries, which are seen as necessities.

Many economic theories try to predict how the consumer will behave; focusing especially on the consumed product that best satisfies the consumer's needs with respect to available income.

The behavior of consumption comprises all the individual acts involved in purchasing and using merchandise and services, including the decision-making processes that precede and determine those acts. Social scientists study both observable and nonobservable behaviors. These behaviors may occur without consumers realizing that they are evaluating alternatives or even making a choice. This process can occur in a split-second or be the result of lifetime of maturation.

The purchase is only one observable step in the consumption process; it is part of decision-making process whose antecedents and consequences must be examined.

The study of consumer behavior determines consumers' perceived needs, how those perceptions are formed, and how they are influenced by marketing. When we talk about marketing, we should recognize that it is about a behavioral process through which millions of individuals are connected by countless institutions.

Consumer behavior is, therefore, a subject encompassing a series of factors: psychological, economic, and social. Human beings are motivated by basic needs and influenced by unique social circumstances that require them to adapt psychologically.

The psychological aspect of consumer behavior is complex, because not all the processes involved in purchasing can be directly observed. Some processes are observable; psychologists have filmed shoppers in stores thousands of times, and some shoppers' actions have been observed through the use of eye-tracking glasses. But other behaviors have been described as belonging to a "black box," driven by mental processes that are variables of concepts like motivation and attitude. The black box can be understood as the center of psychological control, because it includes both the memory and the basic structures of thought and behavior. Personal characteristics and predispositions, information and experiences, and values and attitudes are stored in the memory.

With just a glance, we decide to enter one store instead of another; this explains the accumulation of information that a simple storefront might display to facilitate the decision-making process. Everything we see outside and inside a store will have implications on our purchasing behavior.

Behavior of Consumption

Consumer behavior studies follow the physiological, psychological, and sociological factors that determine consumers' responses and reactions to marketing strategies.

Merchandisers must observe and analyze consumers' decision-making processes—that is, try to explain the reasons for their purchasing behavior, discerning the deep conscious and unconscious motivations that led them to choose a particular product at the point of purchase.

The factors that lead to consumption and therefore underpin decision making can be summarized as follows: habits, impulses, motivation, knowledge, and social pressure. Field research can help explain why consumers react positively or negatively to a particular product in the store.

Each consumer has individual characteristics and needs. Retailers need to observe the types of consumers who frequent their stores, so these consumers can be served in a way that satisfies their needs and emotions. Learning to identify the customer always helps a store sell more.

Most Mass-Merchant Purchase Decisions Are In-Store

The behaviors of mass-merchant shoppers are clearer. In POPAI-USA's 2014 Mass Merchant Study, a continuation of its Shopper Engagement Study series, a key finding is that 82 percent of mass-merchant purchase decisions are made in the store.

POPAI, with the help of Eye Faster, Shopper Sense, and SmartRevenue, sampled almost three thousand shoppers in three major US mass-merchant retail chains. The results from pre- and post-interviews and eye-tracking videos show how the mass-merchant shopper plans shopping trips, navigates through stores, and makes purchase decisions, and what role in-store media play. For instance, 34 percent of mass merchant shoppers do not make any kind of shopping list, compared to the 13 percent of grocery shoppers, which lends to the 62 percent of mass merchant shoppers reporting no use of media from mail, newspapers, circulars, coupons, TV ads, and information from electronics sources to plan their trips. This new insight suggests the importance of persuasive displays in influencing shoppers' purchasing decisions.

Displays have a huge untapped potential to drive unplanned purchases in-store. The eye-tracking part of the POPAI study, conducted by Eye Faster, found that 16 percent of unplanned purchases were driven by a display the shoppers saw during the shopping process.

(www.retailcustomerexperience.com)

Persuasion during the Purchase

There is great controversy about the extent to which advertising and other types of promotions can persuade consumers to use products that they don't need or want. The defenders of free will argue that we cannot teach individuals to like things and purchase them if they do not wish to have them. On the other hand, some research shows that consumers can be taught to want a product that they do not like or need, or that they have no impulse to buy.

Today, there is no doubt that mass advertisements, social media, and in-store communication are vehicles that teach people to have secondary needs they never dreamed of before. The responses to a stimulus to purchase can be simple, such as a reflexive muscle contraction at the sight of chocolate in the supermarket, or it can be complex, such as the doubt generated by facing several options in a drugstore.

Types of Purchase Decisions

There are four types of purchases:
- **Planned purchase** (we already know what we're going to buy before we leave home): This is routine shopping that requires little decision making. Planned purchases are usually low-cost items that do not require the shopper's involvement. If the store does not have a product in stock, the consumer goes to another store or accepts a suggested substitute. Planning a purchase means bringing a list from home. For the majority of shoppers who do not take any list with them, they must see a product in order to remember that they need it. For this reason, retailers assign high importance to the arrangement and separation of products by categories. Consumers of these low-cost items are easily swayed during decision making and often change brands according to promotional materials on gondolas.
- **Generally planned purchase** (we know the type of product we need, but not the specific brand): With this type of purchase, consumers may be familiar with the category, but they'll do some research to find out more about an unknown brand. They tend to be influenced by

merchandising and by the information on the gondola. The display must be convincing so that they don't have to ask the clerk for an opinion. These customers will prefer a better-displayed product with the best price and a known brand. They are generally open to whatever brand and product advantage(s) they recognize first.

- **Important decision purchase** (we need to do deep research before buying): These products are usually unfamiliar or expensive, and buying represents a high risk to the shopper—economically, psychologically, or even in terms of performance. Cars, houses, and more expensive electronics are important decision purchases.
- **Impulse purchase** (we buy something without any planning at all). While passing a store, you decide to step inside and take a quick look, and you end up buying some items because of your own desire. That's an impulse purchase, and it is totally dependent on good merchandising. Well-designed advertising stimulates the impulse purchase and ensures that consumers take advantage of many offers. In-store product displays and careful exposure of promotional materials further increase impulse buying. The same shopper who spends hours trying to decide which computer to buy might buy other products without giving it a second thought. There should be a lot of products spread throughout a store to hook those who are not used to thinking about price before picking something up. Don't think that it is only in this category that people buy on autopilot; some shoppers always operate that way.

The fact that the majority of the stores depend solely on impulse purchases proves the importance of this vast field of merchandising, where in-store promotions attract the attention of anyone who is in doubt during the purchasing process. Usually money is the only factor that restricts impulse purchases.

Impulse buying is an unplanned decision-making process that goes extremely quickly. Shoppers might break their habitual buying pattern because they remember a necessity, find a coupon in their pocket, or remember seeing a commercial featuring the product in question. The impulse may be caused by the shopper's perception of an unknown product as necessary and useful, or it can be part of the shopper's pattern of buying, which leaves the final decision to be made inside the store. In the latter case, there might be some unconscious, latent planning which, encouraged by several stimuli in the store, is expressed by the impulse purchase.

Surveys show that 50 percent of the purchases in self-service stores (supermarkets) are made on autopilot without prior planning when consumers decide within 15 seconds to buy the merchandise only because it is displayed. The aim of an advertisement is to prepare consumers' minds so that they crave the advertised products. But we know that consumers will buy these products only if they find or see them in a store.

Learn how to create that impulse. Try to attract consumers with novelties and honest promotional action that does not cost much.

Self-Service and Hands-On Experience

In many department stores, if you are shopping for cosmetics, you have to go through some steps to touch a product. You need to find the proper counter (products are separated by brand) and ask for someone to help you try on the makeup. At Sephora stores, you can try different things by yourself without feeling guilty or obligated to buy something because someone helped you. Instead of making shoppers try products with the assistance of a salesperson, Sephora stores have cosmetics samples out on the counters, allowing people to wander through at their leisure, trying products at will.

It is important to understand that the products that are put out as samples or demonstrations—that is, the testers—must be obtained from the supplier or be included in the price as part of business. To open products for testing is not a loss, but a decoy. This physical contact with the product is a powerful purchase stimulator. Being able to touch a product or try it on means making a physical connection with it, which predisposes the consumer to buy it. This is a way to cut barriers to the purchase. Free to touch and easy to try on means quick to decide.

Invisible Barriers that Block the Impulse

The product itself is not always responsible for its failure to sell. Almost all the time, it is the environment that surrounds the product that discourages the impulse to purchase. In order to drive more impulse purchases, the store atmosphere and merchandising must undermine consumers' resistance. Many stores fail to detect invisible problems that still register in consumers' subconscious minds, stopping the initial impetus of interest in the product or the store. Many of these invisible barriers are quite simple but negatively affect sales. Here are some of them:

- poor or inconvenient store location
- excessive traffic flow / wrong side of the road
- no space for parking
- uninviting storefront (ugly, dark, too many steps or obstructions)
- disorganized windows or complicated visuals
- shortage or excess of products
- lack of prices in the windows
- confusing arrangements or bad décor
- unreliable tabloids and flyers
- inadequate customer care or unfriendly staff

These problems might seem insubstantial to people who do not understand merchandising, but they may determine the failure or success of a store.

If a salesperson's smile is important, retailers have to assign the same importance to all the visual messages they show. Does this mannequin look friendly, or does she look angry to be there? Try to avoid using forms of communication that could be construed as negative (such as the X in the window), because we are used to avoiding negative signs, just as we do in traffic.

Behavior during Purchases

After entering a store, people tend to walk to the right but look to the left. That's because the majority of the population is right-handed (approximately 90 percent), but we also tend to look the same way that we read, from left to right. Studies suggest that the best place to put products is on the left side of the aisle through which consumers walk. But as consumers tend to cross from one side of the aisle to the other as they come and go, both sides can be well used.

Narrow aisles are used for fast-moving items with small profit margins. Wider aisles slow down consumers and encourage them to look and buy on impulse; these aisles usually contain products with higher margins.

In all types of retail, women circulate a store two times more than men do if that store contains significantly more products for women, families, and children than for men.

A rational purchase decision is based on consideration of the cost-benefit ratio, while an emotional purchase decision is based on feelings of personal pride, style, romance, etc. The purchase decision can be influenced by many other factors, too; it is up to merchandisers to try to lure this "black box"—the mind of the consumer.

What May Affect the Buying Habits?

The following factors affect consumer buying habits:
* promotions
* price tags
* visible quantity
* color and brightness of the display
* promotional materials

Purchase Procedures at POPs

It is necessary to clarify that each type of store has different patterns of purchasing habits. When research of purchase patterns in supermarkets is compared with that of purchase patterns in bakeries, convenience stores, drugstores, etc., it's clear that there are large differences in consumers' interests, habits, and actions depending on the point of purchase. The same person might purchase one way at the supermarket, another way at the convenience store, another way at the bakery, and so on, reflecting several patterns of behavior depending on the type of store. The number of decisions at the point of purchase varies, too, according to the reason for the purchase. It is important to understand that all stores (even in the same chain) have an individual index of decision according to their location, displays, prices, and promotions, as well as the purchasing behavior of their customers.

The difference between consumers and shoppers

Every one of us is a consumer; however, we are not all the same type of shopper. Each of us has categories in which we spend more time and money and categories in which we are trying to spend less time and money. In some categories, we are shopping for ourselves and in some we are buying of others.

Our involvement and engagement in a category as shoppers does not tie neatly to our consumer type. Each individual shopper has different needs, wants, likes and dislikes, so retailers and suppliers need to analyze what decisions are made **pre-store** and what decisions are made **in-store**. The more the retailer is in sync with the manufacturer, the better the manufacturer can create a proper media mix both pre-store and in-store, drive trips and increase sales, quantify the shopper's decisions, and turn that analysis into a profitable outcome for all.

Pre-store and in-store marketing

Because each shopper has her own view on category importance, companies must be aware of which purchases are planned at store level and brand level, and which purchases are not planned at all. Most pre-store decisions are brand driven:

the shopper has purchased the product in the past and will continue to do so in the future. In-store decisions, however, are often based on perceived value, merchandising, and packaging. As a result, promotions and displays are a good investment. Aisle and shelf organization also play a big role in purchasing decisions. It makes sense to organize shelves by brands, but products need to be merchandised in the least confusing way possible. By studying shopper insights, retailers and manufacturers can understand and address the difference between product consideration and product closure.

The old model insufficiently combined market research, marketing, sales, merchandising, operations, and external partners and data sources. A new integrated model is required that is consumer- and shopper- centric, and internally and externally collaborative. With this new model, pre-store and in-store media, marketing, and merchandising can be optimized to increase revenue and profits.

> **"We invest a lot to understand the consumers because even they do not know what they want"**
> **A.G. Lafley, president of Procter & Gamble's administration council**

CHAPTER 10:
TRENDS IN GLOBAL RETAIL

Eye-Tracking Research

Eye tracking is one of the best research methodologies for helping retailers and brands understand the dynamics of consumer behavior.

Eye-tracking research can help explain in-store behavior in general and the dynamics of impulse purchasing specifically. Retailers and brands can use these new insights to gain competitive advantage by developing impulse-purchase-targeted strategies and programs by category and brand.

First, here's some general information about what eye tracking is and what it delivers. The eye-tracker glasses system consists of two cameras that enable researchers to track the following data:

- what people look at (including specific elements on a package), in what order, and for how long
- what people pick up and what parts of the package they look at, in what order, and for how long
- what people put back on the shelf and what they put into their shopping baskets
- how people interact with other people: shoppers, store associates, sales staff

By analyzing this data, retailers and/or manufacturers can answer the following questions:

- What are shoppers seeing?
- What are shoppers not seeing?
- Where do people start their shopping?
- What catches their initial attention?
- How is that attention guided?
- Are certain display elements engaging or confusing?
- Is the intended messaging being conveyed?
- Which packages are picked up?
- What information on the package is evaluated?

- How many products are picked up?
- How many products are purchased, and how many are rejected?
- What did people look at on packages that were purchased and rejected?
- How does interaction with a sales associate influence the purchase decision?

An in-depth interview conducted after the eye-tracking research will reveal the *why* behind the *what* and the *how*.

Researchers use eye-tracking glasses to find out where a shopper's glance falls (the light spots indicate where they glance at and the dark spots indicates where they stare at).

The Consideration Set

The consideration set is the subset of brands a consumer evaluates before making a purchase decision. Getting a brand considered is the prerequisite for its purchase. Consumers' consideration sets include all the products they actively notice in any category in which they make a purchase, planned or on impulse. If a product is not on a consumer's shopping list or kept in mind as a planned purchase, the consumer will only buy it if he or she actively notices it. Shoppers buy only the products that enter their consideration set inside the store.

Consideration sets formed before shoppers get to the store comprise the brands that the shoppers take seriously during purchase decisions—that is, the brands that earned credibility with the shoppers as a result of past usage and consumption experiences.

In the store, however, the consideration set may widen to include any products that catch the attention of the shopper. Attention starts with simply visually noticing a product. Any product looked at long enough could enter the consciousness of the shopper, become part of the consideration set, and influence the purchase decision.

The consideration set is related to, but not the same thing as, mind-share or brand awareness. Mind-share refers to top-of-mind awareness—that is, brands that first come to mind when you think of a product category.

Consumers might remember their favorite brand in a certain category when shopping, and they might even have it on the shopping list (pre-store consideration set), but in the heat of the shopping moment, something else might grab their attention (in-store consideration set) and be purchased. Shoppers' attention could be grabbed by a promotion, price, or new flavor, among other elements.

Eye Tracking and Consideration Set

Consideration set analytics examine the decision-making process, including which and how many other brands shoppers consider for purchase. Mobile eye tracking in-store allows researchers to test which products and brands are in a consumer's wide, intermediate, and narrow consideration sets, which work like a funnel pointing toward the purchase.

Wide consideration set: When a consumer looks or "fixates" longer than 0.3 seconds on a package or certain package components (brand, color, text, image, etc.) without picking the package up. This means the consumer has noticed the product.

Intermediate consideration set: When a consumer fixates longer than 0.5 seconds on a package or certain package components without picking the package up. The consumer is starting to evaluate the product more closely.

Narrow consideration set: When a consumer picks up a package. In this case, the consumer has narrowed down the wider set of products into those that are seriously being considered for purchase.

Here is what researchers have observed and learned about impulse purchasing from thousands of eye-tracking respondents:

1. Notice
The eye tracker records what shoppers see first when approaching a category. Research shows that, typically, left and right ends of shelves serve as visual anchors; shoppers work from the outside in.

Results: Something (a product, a color, a sign, a package, etc.) first attracts shoppers' attention, making them look at it.

2. Evaluate
The difference between noticing and evaluating is the intensity and duration of the shopper's glance. This is when the shopper looks more closely at different shelf areas and several packages in each area. Products that are evaluated are typically in the consideration set for purchase. For this reason, it is important for a product to be easily identified by its package; the product's main benefits should be understood with a few glances.

Results: If the shopper glances at a product and sees anything sale-related, the chance that the product will be picked up is ten times higher than it is if the product doesn't have such a sign.

3. Select

Selection happens when shoppers finally start picking up specific packages and reviewing them in more detail. They make a decision after determining that a certain product fits their purpose and style.

Results: If the price is right, the product tends to be picked up, making the chance of its purchase 90 percent. The product might be checked out in more detail or put straight into the basket.

4. Decide

This is the final split, when the shopper purchases the product and puts it into the shopping basket—or rejects it by putting it back on the shelf. It is critical to understand where shoppers are looking in those final seconds.

Considerations in an Eye-Tracking Study

When conducting an eye-tracking study, it is also important to consider and analyze the following areas because of their potential influence on impulse purchases: type of shopping trip, type of shopper, and product category.

The Type of Shopping Trip Influences Impulse Purchases

- quick trip: to buy certain items (e.g., for dinner that night)
- stock up: weekly shopping trip to stock up the pantry

Shoppers on a quick trip are very task oriented. They want to quickly locate and purchase what they need for dinner. Something that is perceived to fit into that mission can become an impulse purchase. For example, a shopper who wants a rotisserie chicken might pick up a beverage because it is located near the chicken, reminding the shopper that her family also needs a tasty beverage.

Shoppers on stock-up trips are generally open to exploring more because they typically are not under the time pressure of a shopper on a quick trip. They either browse the categories or sections where they are shopping anyway—or they get pulled into the aisles where something interesting has attracted their attention.

Type of shopper influences impulse purchases.
- primary shopper: does the majority of the shopping for the household
- secondary shopper: does a small portion of the shopping for the household

The secondary shopper who is shopping alone is typically in more of a "buying" mode than an "exploration" mode—but during a stock-up trip in the company of the primary shopper, the secondary shopper is more open to exploring and more prone to buying on impulse.

Product category influences impulse purchases.
- fast-moving: snacks and beverages
- slow-moving: household care, body care, dental care, cosmetics
- high involvement: electronics, home appliances

In consumable categories, such as milk, soft drinks, and snacks, shoppers are typically on autopilot, buying what they usually purchase. Something needs to catch their attention to stimulate an impulse purchase—perhaps a new style of packaging or a rearranged shelf. Such categories tend to be very innovative, bringing out lots of new products every year.

High-involvement product areas, where consumers do a lot of preshopping research, are shopped very differently. Shoppers sometimes know more than the store staff and are only in the store to touch and feel or to check out products that are not available online. But a knowledgeable store associate should still be able to change preset minds and decisions, steering customers toward an impulse purchase of a different product that is more expensive, or stimulating some impulse cross-purchases.

It is important to consider past experiences and learning for future studies. Type of shopper, type of shopping trip, and product category clearly have to be considered and analyzed in an eye tracking study for researchers to draw the correct insights and conclusions.

Store Appearance Drives Shopper Attitude

Every shopping trip is different. Consumers' consideration sets change from one trip to the next depending on out-of-store experiences like advertising, social media, friends' statements, etc. But it's also true that the stimuli present in the store change from one shopping trip to the next. The shelves might be organized or messy. There might be new signs or updated price labels. The consumer might be shopping alone or with kids. The shopper's mission might be to find a specific item or to find an item in a general category.

Shelf Placement Drives Purchases

In the first photo below a box of Chocolate Cheerios cereal has a private label cereal placed to the right of it called Toasted Oats that offers a similar flavor. In one study we found many people planned to buy Cheerios specifically but no one mentioned Toasted Oats. After shopping it was discovered that several of those who planned to buy Cheerios noticed the Toasted Oats next to it, looked at both of the prices, discovered that Toasted Oats was cheaper, and choose Toasted Oats instead of Cheerios.

 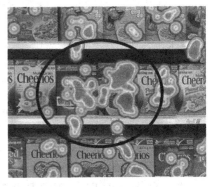

The heat map to the left shows that Toasted Oats got as much attention as the Cheerios next to them on the shelf, and that shoppers examined the price signs for both brands as they compared them.

Leading Brands Do Well in Shelf Blocks

If you are the leading brand, your best strategy is to have a block of space on the shelf so that the cheaper brands are not visually close to your premium brand; this will discourage price comparisons. Remember, you must be a leading brand to use this strategy. In one study, researchers found that Kashi, a healthy cereal brand, was placed in a block across the aisle from the more mainstream cereal brands. There it was getting only minimal attention from shoppers (see photos). Kashi would likely do better if its various cereals were interspersed among the more popular Kellogg's and General Mills products.

A Kashi cereal block (left) gets less attention than the cereals on the other side of the aisle, where Kellogg's and General Mills products are mixed together.

Eye-tracking research can help a brand become the category leader by revealing how the consideration set works in that category. Eye tracking answers the following key questions:

- How many brands and products does a consumer consider in-store?
- Which brands are in competition, and to what extent?
- What products does a particular brand lose sales to?
- What other products are consumers trying/testing?

> *Eye tracking can help shed light on the most important components of impulse purchasing: what is noticed and in what order, and how the shopper reacts as a result.*

Eye tracking can reveal a lot of information and insights that are hidden in plain sight of most other conventional research techniques, like observation and store interviews. Many times people report that shopping a certain category is easy and simple, but eye-tracking research often shows that people have problems that they are not consciously aware of and therefore cannot put into words. People can recall brands they know (awareness), but they can't recall precisely what products they considered when shopping certain categories.

Eye tracking is the only methodology that identifies the consideration set at the shelf inside the retail store. Knowing which other brands are being considered with your brand in-store is the first step to developing a strategy to compete at the retail shelf. Eye tracking can also provide insight into the best shelf placement for a product, whether it is a leading brand or a new entrant.

> *The difference between an impulse purchase and a planned purchase is an outside stimulus that catches the shopper's attention and draws him or her away from the planned shopping path.*

This is a big opportunity for shopper marketing and in-store activation. But before decisions can be made about how to influence impulse purchases, it is important to understand decision processes in more detail.

(Hendrickson, Kirk. "Attention Leads To Action")

The Future of Omni-Channel Retailing

Omni-channel retailing is no longer an option. It must become a part of every retailer's long-term strategy.

Big Data

The amount of information available to retailers is greater than ever before. With omni-channel retailing, stores can gather data at a hyper-granular level. That kind of specificity gives retailers the tools to craft powerful, targeted messaging that drives sales.

Part of that data gathering also includes understanding consumer preferences, whether it is the way people want to purchase their goods, what they prefer in terms of store design, or even how they respond to different scripts that sales associates use on the floor. Because all this data can be tracked, retailers have more knowledge than ever.

It's important for retailers to remember their core mission, audience and products to avoid getting lost in the sea of information that is now available to them.

Showrooming

Part of the challenge for retailers is showrooming—that is, when customers come into the store to decide what product they want to buy and then purchase that product via the Internet. Most retailers cannot compete with the big Internet retailers on price, and attempting to do so leads only to smaller profit margins.

But there is a solution: building relationships.

"Omni-channel retailing is all about creating a one-to-one relationship with millions of people," said Jeff Dickey, managing director of the OmniChannel Marketing Project "Because there are so many touchpoints and so much data and communication data and communication is so much easier, retailers can offer what feels like personal attention to customers, keeping them coming back time and time again."

(Wheeler, E. The Convergence of the Connected Consumer and Omni-Channel Retailing)

Webrooming Eclipses Showrooming

While showrooming remains popular among 76 percent of American consumers, the emerging trend of "webrooming," or researching online before buying in-store, is even more common, representing by 88 percent of shoppers. According to "The Rise of Webrooming: A Changing Consumer Landscape," a report from Interactions, 75 percent of webroomers believe they can find the lowest in-store price, while 72 percent prefer online product comparisons and 71 percent prefer online product research.

The report also highlights why people research in-store before buying online. Sixty-eight percent of respondents said they like to experience the product in person first; 48 percent believe they can find the lowest price online; and 41 percent prefer to seek help from in-store associates during their research process.

Consumers expect retailers to be everywhere they are, so if retailers are not leveraging omni-channel marketing approaches, or not embracing the concept of "everywhere commerce," they risk an inconsistent customer experience, potentially reduced profits, and diminished brand loyalty.

(Berthiaume, Dan. "Webrooming eclipses showrooming")

What started as a fear of cannibalization has evolved into an opportunity for augmentation, as digital and physical convergence accelerates across categories and formats.

The exponential growth of digital has created a retail environment that some years ago did not exist. The retail environment is now a blend of the online and physical world. We've now learned the online experience can't reproduce the physical interaction between consumers and products and now retailers are embracing technology to engage with customers in unique and personalized ways.

All today's customers want price, convenience, offers and individualized services that are as important as to online shoppers. Retail is about offering people the services and products they want – on the devices and media they use. This means that **the customer actually is the store**, which is anytime, anywhere and any device. And we should be prepared for them.

CONCLUSION

To finish, let's think about what it takes for retailers to stay competitive and succeed.

Here's a quick checklist:

1. Be in love with your work, and pass on that attitude to all your employees.
2. Treat your employees like a vital part of your business, because when they are well treated, they treat your customers well, too.
3. Build enduring relationships with your customers, and listen to them every day.
4. Keep and maintain your inventories lean and your presentations clean to let your assortments fresh.
5. Create an honest, inviting store that will be respected in the neighborhood.
6. Treat your suppliers the way you want them to treat you.
7. Don't turn your store into real estate. Your spaces should be used to serve your customers. The extra money might be welcome, but renting space is not your main business.
8. Never humiliate the customers or make shopping difficult; make them feel comfortable - and do not complicate the act of choosing.
9. Control the numbers in your store. If you don't control, you don't know. If you don't know, are you sure you are in the right way to succeed?
10. Try to make your customers smile while they shop.

These are some things we work on with our clients day in and day out. And we don't just use these ideas to reinvigorate and renew stores; we should also continue to observe customers every day to follow any changes in their habits.

Success requires more than merely doing what we've always done. We need to make it better every day.

To make your customers smile, you don't need anything but creativity.

I wish you a happy store.

REFERENCES

Anthony, Mike. "What is the difference between shoppers and consumers?". *Visualise* (Oct 2013). http://www.visualise.ie/what-is-the-difference-between-shoppers-and-consumers-love.

Bernardino, Eliane de Castro; Pacanowski, Mauro; Khoury, Nicolau Elias and Reis, Ulysses Alves dos. *Marketing de Varejo*. São Paulo: Editora FGV, 2006.

Berthiaume, Dan. "Webrooming eclipses showrooming". *Chain Storeage* (May 13, 2014). http://www.chainstoreage.com/article/study-'webrooming'-eclipses-showrooming.

Blessa, Regina. *Merchandising no Ponto de Venda*. São Paulo: Atlas, 2001.

_____. *Merchandising Farma*. São Paulo: Cengage, 2007.

Catalyst. *Catalyst Quick Take: Buying Power*. New York: Catalyst, 2013. http://www.catalyst.org/knowledge/buying-power.

"COR e sua influência na farmácia". *Guia da Farmácia* (Aug 8, 2012). http://guiadafarmacia.com.br/cor-e-sua-influencia-na-farmacia.

Gade, Christiane. *Psicologia do Consumidor e da Propaganda*. São Paulo: EPU, 1998.

Gerrard, Gerry. *"Retail store locations: the science behind the choice"*. *Smart Company* (11 Nov, 2013). www.smartcompany.com.au.

Hammond, Richard. *Smart Retail*. Dorchester: Pearson Education, 2001.

Hendrickson, Kirk. *"Attention Leads To Action"*. *Eye Faster* (2013). http://www.eyefaster.com.

Lima, Manoel Alves, June 7, 2013, comment on Blog da Fal, www. blogdafal.com.br.

Martineau, P.D.: *Motivation and Advertising*. New York: McGraw-Hill, 1948.

Nystrom, Paul Henry. *Fashion merchandising*. New York: The Ronald Press Co, 1932.

POPAI. 2014 *Mass Merchant Study Results*. Chicago: PRWEB, Feb 12, 2014.

Roccato, Pedro L. "Experiência de Compra" (2004). http://www. directchannel.com.br.

Skorupa, Joe. "Optimizing In-Store Merchandising – Part 2: The Store Compliance Challenge". RIS News (2013). http://*www. risnews.edgl.com*.

Spangenberg, Eric R. "Improving the Store Environment: Do Olfactory Cues Affect Evaluations and Behaviors?" *Journal of Marketing*. 60 (1996): 67–80.

Strunck, G. "Antropometria, ergonomia e planogramas". *Mundo do Marketing*. Accessed Jan 5 2015. http://www.mundodomarketing. com.br.

Supermercado Moderno Magazine (Jun 2006).

Wheeler, E. *The Convergence of the Connected Consumer and Omni-Channel Retailing*. Networld Media Group, 2013.

Zmoginski, Felipe. "A Partitura do Varejo." *Guia da Farmácia* (Nov 2006).

**Last photo (the squashes) was taken at
Pão de Açúcar Supermarket -Tremembé - SP (2014).**

Websites

http://www.blessa.com.br
http://www.iev.net.br
http://www.eyefaster.com
http://www.ehow.co.uk
http://retail.about.com
http://www.retailcustomerexperience.com
http://smartrevenue.com
http://www.varejonatv.com.br
http://www.visualise.ie

Regina Blessa is a doctoral researcher at the University of Aveiro, Portugal. She has a master's in Communication from the University of São Paulo, and she majored in Advertising and in Fine Arts. She has postgraduate degrees in Marketing from Columbia University, in Communication from New York University, and in Administration from Fundação Getúlio Vargas in São Paulo, Brazil.

A pioneer in merchandising in Brazil, Regina Blessa is a passionate professor, consultant, speaker, and trainer who has helped countless businesses discover new opportunities at the point of purchase and achieve better brand returns. After a consumer goods career spanning 23 years, Regina redirected his energy and enthusiasm toward founding IEV, a retail studies institute that leverages the power of merchandising, shopper marketing and customer management to clients and students. As the institute's CEO, Regina has worked with the world's leading companies, such as Pfizer, Bayer, Sanofi, Coca Cola, Johnson and Johnson, Walmart, Carrefour, Nestlé, Siemens, Kellogg's, Takeda, Abbott, Merck, Colgate, Novartis, Boehringer and Cencosud.

Blessa participated in the foundation of the Brazilian chapter of POPAI as vice president of training and is professor at Fundação Getúlio Vargas, Senac and other universities. Blessa has published two bestsellers in Brazil, Merchandising no PDV (2001) and Merchandising Farma (2007), and she is a regular columnist for retail industry magazines.

Contact Regina Blessa: reginablessa@gmail.com
www.no-failretail.com

Printed in the United States
By Bookmasters